Contents

KU-677-826

Introduction

Everybody has heard of Poland, the large country wedged sometimes uncomfortably between the Russia-dominated east and Germany to the west. Waves of mass emigration mean that Poles can be found everywhere. Yet how many of us can say we truly know the country itself, its superb cuisine, the warm hospitality of its people, the magical alpine scenery of its southern reaches or the grandeur of its historical towns and cities?

Although Warsaw and Kraków are now well-established city-break destinations, this country still keeps much of its treasure under wraps, undiscovered in rural corners of the provinces where tourists are thin on the ground, or even in the middle of cities that have hundreds of thousands of inhabitants, but which many in the West have never even heard of. Come and discover Poland – take a journey into the country's turbulent history, admire the resilience and independence of its people, and stand back in awe of its culture.

Who are the Poles? Although a mix of Slavs, Germans, Scandinavians, Lithuanians, Ukrainians and possibly many others, they are quite distinct from their neighbours in culture, religious devotion and genuine hospitality. They take a real interest in foreigners who visit their country, making travel in Poland a rewarding experience. The Poles can very often be a romantic dreamy nation, at other times pragmatic and businesslike. Polish society has many influences – possibly the strongest is the Catholic Church, and the Poles are one of the most devout nations in Europe, with a high percentage of even young people attending church on a regular basis. The upheaval and horrors of World War II still live in the national psyche, as do the years spent under martial law in the early 1980s. However, the Poles are a resilient nation and are determined to make their country into a European success story, while not forgetting their recent past.

Those who travelled in Poland before 1989 will hardly recognise the country these days. It has lost a lot of its drabness and uniformity, with unbridled capitalism bringing colour to the streets, and newly found funds bringing renovation to its tourist attractions. Cafés, bars and restaurants abound in the cities, while out in the countryside visitors can still experience the unchanging, timeless

TRAVELLERS

POLAND

WITHDRAWN

By
MARC DI DUCA

Written and updated by Marc Di Duca
Original photography by Marc Di Duca and Christopher Holt

Published by Thomas Cook Publishing
A division of Thomas Cook Tour Operations Limited.
Company registration no. 1450464 England
The Thomas Cook Business Park, Unit 9, Coningsby Road,
Peterborough PE3 8SB, United Kingdom
E-mail: books@thomascook.com, Tel: + 44 (0) 1733 416477
www.thomascookpublishing.com

Produced by Cambridge Publishing Management Limited
Burr Elm Court, Main Street, Caldecote CB23 7NU

ISBN: 978-1-84848-005-6

First edition © 2007 Thomas Cook Publishing
This second edition © 2009
Text © Thomas Cook Publishing
Maps © Thomas Cook Publishing/PCGraphics

Series Editor: Maisie Fitzpatrick
Production/DTP: Steven Collins

Printed and bound in Italy by Printer Trento

Cover photography: Front L-R: © Cozzi Guido/4Corners Images;
© Kevin Foy/Alamy; © Gusso Luca/4Corners Images
Back: © Robert Harding Picture Library/Alamy

The Polish coat of arms

tranquillity of the land, and witness a mini-renaissance in folk culture. Travel is now much easier than it once was as the infrastructure is gradually improving (with the exception of the roads). Hotels have improved immensely with major centres offering the full range of accommodation, including 5-star luxury. Information is easy to come by, and the tourist infrastructure in many places is well advanced.

Poland can provide a rewarding, entertaining and relaxing holiday for anyone. Come and hike the mountain trails, visit the opera, tour the old streets of medieval cities, watch wildlife in the national parks, and enjoy the sandy beaches. In the evening, retire to cosy pubs and restaurants to enjoy some of the best cuisine in Central and Eastern Europe, washed down with fine vodka and excellent beers. Then enjoy a concert, a folk night or an evening at the opera. There's something for everybody in this big chunk of Europe.

The land

Poland is one of the largest countries in Europe at 312,685sq km (120,728sq miles), of which 8,220sq km (3,174sq miles) is made up of lakes and rivers. According to estimates from mid-2006, there are just over 38.5 million people living in Poland. The country can be divided into four distinct areas: the mountains in the south, the vast central plain, the lake belt, and the coastline in the north.

As far as landscapes go, Poland has it all. The snowcapped Tatra and rounded Sudeten Mountains form the southern borders with the Czech Republic and Slovakia. These give way to the flat plains of the central lowlands with their rolling agricultural landscapes and fertile soils. Next come the lakes (Poland has the most lakes of any European country bar Finland), formed by a glacier 10,000 years ago. In the far north, sandy beaches and shifting dunes line the Baltic Sea.

Northeast Poland

The northeast of the country, bordering on Belarus, the Russian enclave of Kaliningrad and Lithuania, is made up of the historical territories of Masuria, Warmia, Podlasie and Mazovia. To the north, this is a region of lakes, rivers, swamps and wetlands with ample opportunity for water-sports in the summer. Poland's largest lake, Lake Śniardwy, can be found in the centre of the Great Masurian Lakes area, which also boasts some dense forest land. Mazovia is archetypal rural plain country, while Podlasie is known for its forests and the Białowieża National Park.

Małopolska and the Carpathian Mountains

Małopolska, which borders on Ukraine in the east, is a huge area of rolling green hills, fertile plains and agricultural land. This scene is only interrupted by the Małopolska Uplands around Kielce and the Sandomierz Valley. To the south rise the Carpathian Mountains arching across the bottom of the country. Poland's highest mountain, Rysy (2,499m/8,200ft), can be found in the Tatra National Park near the town of Zakopane.

Pomerania and Wielkopolska

Pomerania is the region of Poland bordering Germany to the west and the Baltic Sea to the north. The coast is a dramatic place of shifting sand dunes, endless white sandy beaches and stormy seas. Inland, there are the lakes of the Kashubian Region. Wielkopolska, up against the frontier with Germany, is a largely flat region dotted with forests and lakes.

Silesia

The historical territory of Silesia, against the border with the Czech Republic, can be found in the far southwestern corner of the country. To the south, there are the ancient Sudeten Mountains, the best-known range being the Karkonosze. The highest mountain in the Sudeten Mountains is Śnieżka at 1,602m (5,256ft) above sea level.

Climate

Poland's climate is affected by maritime influences from Western Europe and a continental climate coming in from the east. Add to this polar air from Scandinavia and subtropical air occasionally wafting over the mountains from the south and the picture is a pretty mixed bag. The south has a more continental climate, while the north's weather is affected by its proximity to the sea.

The land

The rooftops of Kazimierz Dolny in southeastern Poland

The land

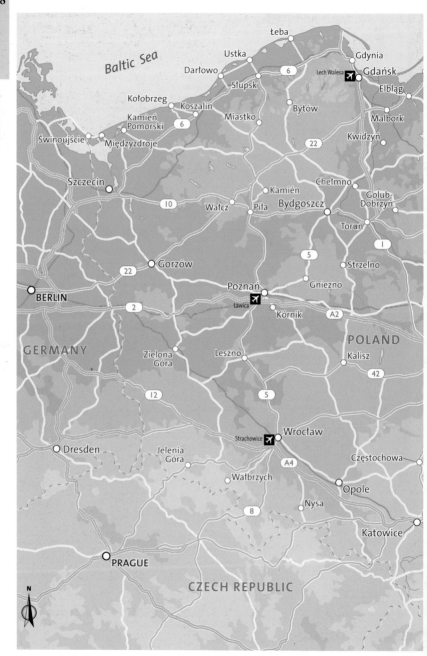

History

10th century The area around Poznań on the Warta River is settled by the Polanie tribe (hence Poland), led by Piast, who unites the scattered Slav clans into a single unit.

1038 Kraków is established as capital.

1226 Teutonic Knights conquer northern Poland from their base at Malbork Castle.

1320 The Polish crown is restored and the Polish state reunified under Kazimierz III Wielki.

1364 Kazimierz III Wielki founds Kraków University.

1382 Poles form a dynastic alliance with Lithuania. Beginning of the Jagiellonian dynasty's reign.

1506–72 Poland's Renaissance golden age – the arts flourish under Kings Zygmunt I Stary and Zygmunt II August and there is widespread religious tolerance.

1569 Poland unites with Lithuania to form the largest state in Europe at the time.

1596–1609 The capital is moved from Kraków to Warsaw by King Zygmunt III Waza.

1655–60 Swedish invasion known as the Deluge. Plague, wars, famine and invaders eat away at the country and its population.

1772 Prussia, Russia and Austria annex 30 per cent of Polish territory in the so-called First Partition of Poland.

1791 Poland acquires a written constitution, only the second in the world after the USA.

1793 Second Partition – Russia and Prussia seize another 50 per cent of Polish territory.

1795 Third Partition – Poland is divided up in its entirety between the three major powers, and disappears from the map of Europe for over 120 years.

19th century	Period of armed rebellions, Russian oppression and mass emigration to the New World.
1914–18	Poland witnesses fierce fighting during World War I.
1918	Marshal Józef Piłsudski declares himself head of an independent Polish state.
1919–20	Polish–Soviet War won by forces commanded by Piłsudski. Poland acquires territory in what is now Ukraine and Belarus.
1922	Piłsudski resigns but returns four years later in a military coup. He rules as dictator until his death in 1935.
1939	Hitler and Stalin secretly agree to divide up Poland between them. The Nazis invade on 1 September and overrun the country, starting World War II. Soviets invade from the east on 17 September.
1941	Following Hitler's attack on the Soviet Union, the Nazis drive the Red Army out of eastern Poland.
1941–5	The concentration camps at Oświęcim (Auschwitz) and Treblinka witness the worst atrocities of the Holocaust. Poland's 3 million Jews are murdered en masse.
1943	Around 50,000 Jews, all that remain of the Warsaw ghetto of around half a million, revolt against the Nazis in the Ghetto Uprising.
1944	With the Red Army liberating cities to the east, Warsaw rises against the Nazis. The Red Army holds back from Warsaw in order to allow the Germans to defeat the Poles, thus eradicating any nationalist resistance to a communist takeover.
1945	The Red Army marches into Warsaw. Only 15 per cent of Warsaw's buildings remain standing at the end of the war. Six million Poles lie dead. The Yalta Conference defines Poland's new borders, effectively shifting the country further west. Poland comes under the USSR's sphere of influence.

1947	The Communist Party wins a flawed general election. A period of Stalinism and Sovietisation follows. The Church, however, remains a significant force in Polish society.
1953	Stalin dies. Political oppression eases somewhat in Poland.
1970	Riots break out in Gdańsk, Gdynia and Szczecin following price rises. Forty-four people die.
1970s	Polish economy goes into freefall.
1978	Karol Wojtyła, archbishop of Kraków, becomes Pope John Paul II.

Pope John Paul II

1980	The Solidarity Movement is founded. Lech Wałęsa, an electrician from the Gdańsk shipyard, becomes its chairman. Strikes are held to call for political reform.
1981	General Jaruzelski declares martial law across Poland. Solidarity is officially suspended.
1985	Gorbachev becomes president of the USSR, ushering in a new era of *glasnost* and *perestroika*.
1989	Round Table Agreements between Church, opposition and state leads to semi-democratic elections, the first in the Eastern Bloc.
1990	The Communist Party is dissolved. Free-market reforms are launched. Lech Wałęsa becomes president.
2004	Poland joins the European Union (EU). Many young Poles immediately leave to work in the UK and Ireland.
2012	Poland set to co-host football's European Championships with Ukraine.

Famous Poles

Every country has a list of its illustrious sons and daughters, and Poland is no exception. In relation to its size, this country has given the world many famous names, some excelling in the fields of science and literature, others bringing change and peace to a turbulent region. The Poles like to remember their most celebrated countrymen and women with statues, street names and museums.

Perhaps the most famous Pole of our time was Pope John Paul II, born **Karol Józef Wojtyła** in Wadowice in southern Poland in 1920. He was the

Frederyk Chopin

first non-Italian pope in 450 years and a thorn in the side of the Polish communists from 1978 when he was elected. Indeed, he was instrumental in ending communism in Poland and across Eastern Europe.

Many will know **Lech Wałęsa**, born in 1943 in Popowo near Włocławek, as the leader of the Solidarity Movement in the 1980s. He was awarded the Nobel Peace Prize in 1983 and later served as Polish president.

Marie Curie, born Marie Skłodowska in Warsaw in 1867, managed to excel in the male-dominated world of science. With her husband, she isolated the elements polonium and radium and won the Nobel Prize for Physics and Chemistry. Another famous Polish scientist was **Nicolaus Copernicus**, born in Toruń in 1473, who first stated that the earth orbited the sun.

Adam Mickiewicz (poet), **Frederyk Chopin** (composer) and **Joseph Conrad** (writer; real name Jósef Teodor Konrad Korzeniowski) are all great figures from the world of culture. The film director **Roman Polański** was born in Paris to Polish parents and grew up in Poland during World War II.

Politics

The Republic of Poland has seen great political changes since the fall of the communist system in 1989. Democratic, free and fair elections have been held regularly in the intervening years, with a series of coalitions holding sway in the Sejm, the Polish parliament in Warsaw. Poland operates a bicameral system with elections to an upper chamber (Senat) taking place every four years.

The country's president is head of state and is directly elected by the people for a five-year term, and for a maximum of ten years. The current president is Lech Kaczyński from the conservative Law and Justice Party, whose identical twin brother Jarosław served as prime minister from 2006 to 2007. The incumbent prime minister is Donald Tusk of the Citizens' Platform Party.

The Polish political scene

Throughout the 1990s, various coalitions formed centre-left and centre-right governments and, despite corruption and sleaze allegations, these advanced the reform process started in 1990 and led the country to NATO and EU membership. In September 2005, new elections were held that saw the end of four years of centre-left supremacy. A new right-wing coalition was formed between the Law and Justice Party, the Self-Defence Party and the League of Polish Families.

This, however, broke down in September 2006 over a row about Poland's involvement in Afghanistan, and in 2007 the Citizens' Platform Party under Donald Tusk won a general election.

Political parties

Poland has numerous political parties, but the biggest are the Law and Justice Party (PiS), the Citizens' Platform (PO), the Democratic Left Alliance (SLD), the Self-Defence Party (*Samoobrona*), the League of Polish Families (LPR) and the Polish Peasants' Party (PSL). It is very difficult to divide some of these neatly into left and right, and most defy any classic definition. Most parties appeal to either city dwellers or rural communities, illustrating the immense economic difference between these two groups in society. The Catholic Church also plays a major role in the policy-making decisions of several parties. The Law and Justice Party, which currently dominates the Polish political scene, could be said to stem from the Solidarity Movement of the 1980s. The SLD is what remains of the Communist Party, although this is now a progressive liberal grouping. One of the most extreme parties is the right-wing nationalist League of Polish Families which opposed Poland's accession into the EU, supports a high level of government intervention in the economy, and protects 'traditional' values such as pro-life policies and religion.

Society

Most people in post-communist Poland remain fairly sceptical about politics and see corruption as the key challenge. Recent problems such as the resignation of the prime minister in 2006 following a rift with his party have only exacerbated public despair with politicians and will certainly lead to further disengagement, of young people in particular, in the political process. Poland is no exception in this respect in the Central and Eastern European region. Membership of the EU, Poland's relationships with Germany and Russia, and the country's communist past are still political hot potatoes. However, most people are probably concerned with Poland's more immediate problems such as crippling unemployment and the state of the nation's roads.

Round Table talks in 1989 led to semi-democratic elections

Culture

Poles are an incredibly cultured and well-read people who can put many Westerners to shame with their knowledge of world literature, opera and classical music. Even small towns have art galleries, and major cities such as Warsaw, Kraków, Wrocław and Gdańsk enjoy vibrant opera, jazz and classical music scenes.

Music

One figure overshadows all others in the world of Polish classical music – the pianist and composer Frederyk Chopin (1810–49). Born in Żelazowa Wola near Warsaw to a Polish mother and French father (hence his French surname), Chopin went on to become a child prodigy and, after moving to Paris, a celebrated composer. He took much of his inspiration from Polish folk music. Other 19th-century Polish composers who enjoy less fame abroad are Stanisław Moniuszko (1819–72) and Henryk Wieniawski (1835–80), and, from the 20th century, music by Karol Szymanowski (1882–1937) is worth seeking out.

Opera is popular in big cities, and don't be surprised to see many young

Folk art figures in Sromów (*see p57*)

people filing into theatres, especially in cities with large student populations. Tickets are cheap and performances highly recommended.

Jazz is surprisingly in demand in Poland, and has been since the 1950s when it started as an underground movement. Most large towns have at least one jazz venue, and the standard of performances is high.

There has been something of a revival in folk music in recent years, with events such as the International Festival of Mountain Folklore and other folk festivals attracting younger audiences tired of bland Western pop. The best places to hear folk music are the mountainous regions of the south and southeast, and the rural areas of the east.

Western pop music is fashionable in Poland, but local efforts leave much to be desired. Polish hip-hop, which tries to mimic rap artists from the West, is particularly dreadful.

Painting

Polish painters to look out for in galleries across the country are Jan Matejko (1838–93), Wojciech Kossak (1857–1942), Stanisław Wyspiański (1869–1907), Olga Boznańska (1865–1940), Jacek Malczewski (1854–1929), Tadeusz Makowski (1882–1932) and Tadeusz Kulisiewicz (1899–1988). Jan Matejko is perhaps the best known, and his works can be found in almost every major gallery in the country.

Teatr Studio in Warsaw

Folk art

Many people in the south and east of Poland are keen to keep Poland's rich folk traditions alive. Away from ethnographic museums, folk dress and art can be seen at religious feasts and folk festivals, as well as at *skansens* (open-air museums).

Literature

Poland has rarely set the literary world alight, and most outside the country would be hard pushed to name a famous Polish writer or poet. Within Poland, romantic poet Adam Mickiewicz (1798–1855) and novelist Henryk Sienkiewicz (1846–1916) are the giants of the book world. Joseph Conrad was born in what was Poland before World War II (now Ukraine), and Günter Grass was a native of Gdańsk.

Festivals and events

Throughout the year, Polish towns and cities host a plethora of festivals and events, from medieval pilgrimages to smoky jazz sessions, and from thigh-slapping folk bashes to high-brow classical music performances. Summer and autumn are the best time to catch musical events, but religious festivals, of which Poland has many, happen throughout the year.

Catholic festivals

Almost every month sees one religious festival or another celebrated across Poland. All Saints' Day (1 November), Easter and Holy Week (March or April), St John's Day (24 June), St Anne's Day (26 July) and the Feast of the Assumption (15 August) are just a few of the biggest occasions that see churches packed to the rafters, processions bearing crosses and flowers, and various other activities and ceremonies steeped in religious symbolism and tradition. Many are used as an excuse to party in the streets and can be a lot of fun.

Chopin Competition

Only held every five years, this is Poland's most prestigious classical music event. The next competition will be in 2010. *www.chopin.pl*

Jazz festivals

Jazz is popular across Poland, and many towns and cities hold annual jazz events. The Poznań Jazz Festival (March), the Warsaw Summer Jazz Days (July/August) and the Kraków Summer Jazz Festival (July/August) are the best known.

June

Kazimierz Dolny Folk Festival This festival takes place outdoors on the Renaissance market square in the picturesque town of Kazimierz Dolny in southeast Poland. For three days the square comes alive with the sounds and colour of traditional folk ensembles from around the country.

June/July

Jewish Culture Festival Held in Kraków for the first time in 1988, this festival of Jewish culture has grown into one of the largest events of its kind in the world. Every year there are over 100 events involving dozens of performers and thousands of participants from across the globe. The climax is the 'Shalom on ulica

Szeroka', a concert attended by around 13,000 people.
www.jewishfestival.pl

Warsaw Mozart Festival Only begun in 1991 to mark the 200th anniversary of Mozart's death, this festival has taken place every year since, and sees performances of all of Mozart's operas and a selection of his chamber, symphonic and vocal-instrumental works. These are all performed by the Warsaw Chamber Opera, the only company in the world to have such a repertoire.
www.operakameralna.pl

August

Dominican Fair in Gdańsk This fair was first held in 1260 by the local monks and has grown into the city's largest annual festival. First held on the small Plac Dominikański, it has now spread out to occupy much of the Main Town. A thousand stalls are crammed into Gdańsk's old streets and squares and along the waterfront, and there are round-the-clock performances, rock and pop concerts, firework displays, sports contests and events to suit every age and interest.
www.mtgsa.pl

International Festival of Mountain Folklore Folk ensembles from mountainous regions all over the world (the majority from Europe) gather in Zakopane in the Tatra Mountains for several days of music and dance every year in late August. An amazingly vibrant event and most of the performances are free.
www.zakopane.pl

A folk festival in Kraków

Highlights

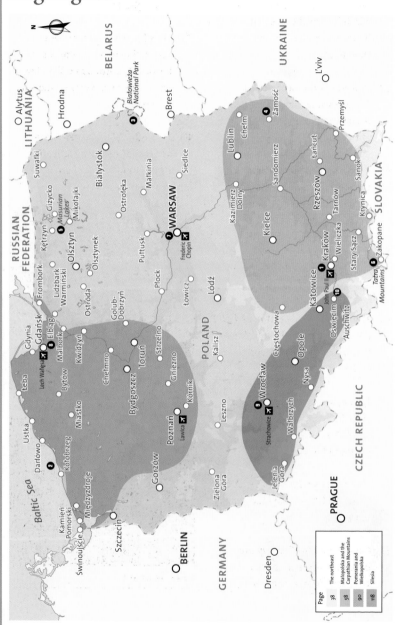

❶ Kraków Poland's best-preserved historical centre, the highlight of which is Wawel Castle, an important symbol of Polish statehood.

❷ Beaches of the Baltic coast Endless white, sandy stretches of beach and the largest sand dunes in Europe.

❸ Białowieża National Park Bison-spotting in Poland's oldest national park on the Belarusian border.

❹ Zamość A perfect example of a late 16th-century Renaissance town and a UNESCO-listed site.

❺ Masurian Lakes An area of 4,000 lakes in northeast Poland, ideal for anglers and watersports enthusiasts.

❻ Hiking in the Tatra Mountains Walk the many trails crisscrossing one of the most picturesque ranges in the Carpathians.

❼ Warsaw Poland's capital with its pretty Old Town and modern city centre.

❽ Gdańsk and the Tri-City area Enjoy the diversity of the Tri-City – from Gdańsk's Main Town, to Sopot's beaches and nightlife.

❾ Wrocław The city's student population and the renovated historical centre make Wrocław one of the most vibrant cities in the country.

❿ Oświęcim (Auschwitz) Learn about the horrors of the most infamous of all the Nazi concentration camps.

Gdańsk waterfront

Suggested itineraries

What you see in Poland very much depends on how much time you have. Poland has enough tourist attractions, historical town centres, castles, national parks and places of natural beauty to keep a visitor occupied for several months of non-stop travel. You probably won't have that much time at your disposal, so here are a few ideas of places to visit on a tight schedule.

Long weekend

The ideal long weekend (four days) in Poland would see you spend two days touring the wonders of historical Kraków, then catching the train to Warsaw to spend the remaining time strolling around the Old Town and admiring the view from the top of the Palace of Culture and Science. You might even squeeze in a trip to the Łazienki Park in Warsaw or the Wieliczka Salt Mines near Kraków.

One week

Two itineraries come to mind with one week to fill. The first involves a start in Kraków from where trips to Oświęcim (Auschwitz) and the Wieliczka Salt Mines are feasible. Then catch an express train to Warsaw, spend a few days in the Old Town, and head out east to the Białowieża National Park. The second route leads from Gdańsk, visiting Poznań and Wrocław en route to the mountains of the south.

Two weeks

With two weeks to kill, start your journey in Gdańsk on the north coast, then head east via Malbork Castle to the Masurian Lake District. From there, it's south all the way to Kraków, taking in the Białowieża National Park

Misty morning in Warsaw

and Warsaw along the way. From Kraków you can make trips to Oświęcim (Auschwitz) and the Wieliczka Salt Mines.

Longer visits

Those lucky enough to have a month on their hands could make a grand tour of Poland's sights, including some lesser-known places and rarely explored regions. Starting in Gdańsk, explore the city then head out along the Baltic coast to the Hel Peninsula and the Słowiński National Park. Travel to Poznań via Malbork Castle and Toruń, and from there make day trips to Rogalin and Kórnik castles. Continue south to explore the Karkonosze Mountains on the Czech border, and then travel to one of Silesia's most important cities, Wrocław. From here, pass quickly through the industrial regions of the south, perhaps stopping off in Katowice, until you reach Oświęcim (Auschwitz) for a tour of the concentration camp. Zakopane and the Tatra National Park lie just 64km (40 miles) to the southeast, and after a few days hiking the mountain trails there, hop on a train to Kraków, which warrants a minimum of three days with at least one day at the Wieliczka Salt Mines. The rarely visited southeast should be your next destination, ending up in the Renaissance town of Zamość. After this, Warsaw should be your next stop. Spend at least three days enjoying the sophistication of the capital before heading east to the Białowieża National Park to do some bison-spotting. From the Belarusian border, make your way lazily up to the Great Masurian Lakes where you can round off your Polish epic with some messing around on the water.

The Tatra National Park near Zakopane

Warsaw

At first sight this city holds few attractions, with its soulless high-rise city centre and three-lane motorways carving up the city. But all that will change once you have visited the rebuilt Old Town, the Uprising Museum and the Palace of Culture and Science, learning more about the resilience of its inhabitants during World War II.

Respite from the city comes in the form of Łazienki Park to the south, at the end of the former Royal Way leading from the Royal Palace in the Old Town. As the capital of Poland, Warsaw is also a major cultural centre, has some of the country's finest restaurants and cafés, and is

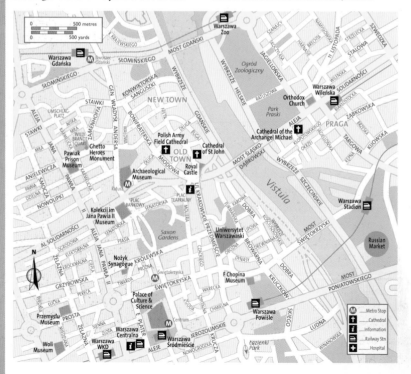

a venue for all kinds of musical and sporting events.

Orientation

As far as visitors are concerned, the sprawling city centre is divided into two distinct areas. The Old Town and the small so-called New Town are to the north on the left bank of the Vistula River. To the south lies the modern city centre. Across the river is the seldom-visited Praga district. The rest – endless hectares of faceless dormitory blocks extending for kilometres in every direction – is of no interest whatsoever to the tourist. Getting around Warsaw is thankfully made easy by a well-regimented public transport system. Visitors will mostly use the trams and buses and, perhaps on rare occasions, the metro, which has only one line, running north–south.

History

Warsaw was hardly on the map up until the 15th century, when it became the capital of the Duchy of Mazovia. In 1569, following the union between Poland and Lithuania, the Polish parliament was moved to Warsaw, but the history of Warsaw as the capital of Poland begins in 1596 when King Sigmund III moved his court from far-flung Kraków. The division of Poland at the end of the 18th century meant that Warsaw found itself in the Russian-dominated east. During the 19th century, Warsaw became a provincial town and an outpost of the Russian Empire. After World War I, Warsaw once again became the capital of newly independent Poland. World War II changed everything and was the greatest tragedy the city ever witnessed. The Germans occupied the city in September 1939, and over the next six years the Jews were forced into the ghetto, hundreds of thousands were shot, the ghetto rose up against the Nazis, and the populace then tried to defeat the occupiers in the doomed Warsaw Uprising. An irate Hitler ordered the German army to raze the city to the ground as punishment for the revolt. Warsaw was finally

(*cont on p28*)

Mermaid statue, Old Town Square

Walk: Old Warsaw

This stroll through Warsaw's rebuilt Old and New Towns passes all the major sights in this part of the city.

Allow 2–3 hours minimum.

Starting in the Old Town on triangular Castle Square with its statue of Polish King Sigmund Vasa III, the first building you will notice on the right is the Royal Castle.

1 Royal Castle

Originally built in the 14th century, the castle served as a royal residence and the Polish parliament. On Hitler's orders it was destroyed after the Warsaw Uprising, but rebuilt in the 1970s and 1980s using money donated from Poles abroad. The magnificent interiors full of original period furniture and works of art can be visited on a guided tour.
Plac Zamkowy 4.
Tel: 022 35 55 170.
www.zamek-krolewski.com.pl.
Open: Tue–Sat 10am–4pm, Sun 11am–4pm.
Continuing northwest along Świętojańska Street, you will soon see the red-brick Gothic façade of the Cathedral of St John on the right.

2 Cathedral of St John

The original cathedral stood here in the 14th century and was added to over the centuries. Almost totally destroyed in World War II, it was rebuilt in its purest Gothic form. The simple interior is illuminated by some wonderful modern stained-glass windows.

Turn right onto Świętojańska Street and after 100m (110yds) you will reach the centrepiece of the historical district, the Old Town Square.

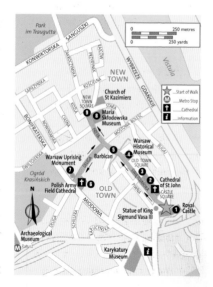

3 Old Town Square

This square, lined on all sides with three- to six-storey town houses, has a small-town atmosphere and is the prettiest place in Warsaw. Activity centres on the photogenic statue of a mermaid, the symbol of Warsaw, dating from 1855. The tables of street cafés spill out onto the cobbles of the square, and pigeons peck around the feet of the numerous sightseers.

Knights' Hall, Royal Castle

4 Warsaw Historical Museum

The northern flank of the Old Town Square is occupied by a museum that traces the history of Warsaw from its very beginnings to the present day. *Rynek Starego Miasta 28. Tel: 022 635 16 25. www.mhw.pl. Open: Tue–Thur 11am–6pm, Wed, Fri 10am–3.30pm, Sat–Sun 10.30am–4.30pm. Admission charge.*
Leave the Old Town Square via Świętojańska Street and head northwest to the Barbican.

5 Barbican

The Barbican was built in 1548, and the town walls on either side are still being renovated.
Having passed through the Barbican, you are now in the so-called New Town. Turn left into Długa Street and the cathedral is on the left at the end.

6 Polish Army Field Cathedral

The building dates from 1642 and has been associated with the army since 1920. The anchor and propeller in front of the cathedral are symbols of the armed forces.

7 Warsaw Uprising Monument

Almost opposite the cathedral stands the evocative monument to the Warsaw Uprising, an impressive chunk of socialist realism. Bronze members of the resistance charge out from beneath huge concrete slabs jutting into the sky, and one is caught emerging from a manhole. *Retrace your steps back along Długa Street and turn left onto Freta Street. The Maria Skłodowska Museum is on the right.*

8 Maria Skłodowska Museum

This is a small museum dedicated to Maria Skłodowska-Curie. *ul. Freta 16. Tel: 022 831 80 92. www.ptchem.lodz.pl. Open: Tue–Sat 10am–4pm, Sun 10am–2pm. Admission charge. Free on Thur. Turn right out of the museum and Freta Street leads to the New Town Square.*

9 New Town Square

This tranquil piazza is dominated by the attractive snow-white Church of St Kazimierz.

liberated by the Red Army in January 1945, although there was little left standing to free from German control. Buildings in the Old and New Towns were meticulously rebuilt, and a brave new city centre was constructed from the communists' favourite building material – reinforced concrete.

SOUTH OF THE OLD TOWN
Plac Bankowy

Senatorska Street continues from Plac Teatralny west to busy Plac Bankowy. The name betrays the occupants of the square – former financial institutions – as this used to be the hub of the financial district in the 19th century. The western flank of the square is dominated by the **City Hall**, which has been the seat of the city council since 1947. The former building of the National Bank next door now houses the **John Paul II Collection** of art, including works by Van Gogh, Renoir, Rubens and many others. The huge blue skyscraper to the north, dating from the early 1970s, was built on the site of the Great Synagogue and is said to be cursed as a result.

Horse and carriage rides in the Old Town Square

Plac Teatralny

A short distance along Senatorska Street from Castle Square you will find wide, palace-lined Theatre Square. As the name suggests, the square is home to the neoclassical **Grand Theatre**, dating from 1825. This is one of Europe's largest theatres with almost 2,000 seats, and it hosts regular performances by the National Opera as well as ballet.

Two palaces dominate the rest of Theatre Square: the **Jabłonowski Palace** opposite the theatre dates from the late 18th century and served as Warsaw's town hall until 1817; the mid-18th-century **Blank Palace** is named after a banker of that name who owned the building from 1777.

The Saxon Gardens

The Saxon Gardens extend southeast from Plac Bankowy. As with so many gardens around Europe, they were based on the gardens at Versailles, and date from the early 18th century. This was the first public park created for the citizens of Warsaw. The park contains numerous pieces of sculpture, over 100 species of tree, a fountain pool and Warsaw's first water tower built in the mid-19th century. At the eastern end you will find the Tomb of the Unknown Soldier, all that remains of a royal residence called the Saxon Palace which was destroyed by the Nazis and never rebuilt.

The castle at the end of Royal Way

ul. Krakowskie Przedmieście

This long, wide street leads from Castle Square south until it meets Świętokrzyska where it becomes Nowy Świat. This is the Royal Way, leading from the castle to Łazienki Park. The first place of interest is immediately to the left – the **Church of St Anne** – alongside its freestanding belfry,

(cont on p32)

The Warsaw Uprising

One of the greatest acts of resistance against the Nazis in all occupied Europe was the Warsaw Uprising, which began on 1 August 1944. The Armia Krajowa (AK) was the largest resistance movement in Europe with over 400,000 members, and their decision to launch a full-on attack was triggered by the arrival of the first Red Army tanks on the left bank of the Vistula River. The AK wanted to rid Warsaw of the Nazis, but was fearful and mistrustful of the Soviets too as the Red Army had detained AK units in the territories it had liberated to the east. The AK desperately wanted to establish an independent government before Poland came under Stalin's sphere of influence.

It was perhaps for this reason that the uprising was doomed from the start. The Soviets had no intention of assisting the AK and would let the stronger Nazis defeat them before moving in to claim the city. AK commander Tadeusz Komorowski

Two groups of figures feature in the Uprising Monument: this is 'Insurgents' …

sprang a surprise assault on Warsaw city centre on 1 August, and for several days the AK enjoyed success. However, under General von dem Bach-Zelewski, the Nazis had air power on their side and began to retake sections of the city, massacring the local population as they went. Eight thousand people were murdered in the Wola district, while in Ochota 40,000 were butchered as the AK retreated.

By late August, the AK occupied just a small section of the Old Town. The choice was either escape or death at the hands of the Nazis, so on 2 September around 2,000 AK insurgents descended into the sewers to make their getaway, entering through a single manhole on Krasiński Square. Skirmishes went on until 2 October when Komorowski and his troops surrendered. By the end of the uprising, 20,000 AK troops were dead, and an incredible 225,000 civilians had been killed.

That was not the end of the matter as far as the Germans were concerned, and an incensed Hitler immediately ordered the complete destruction of Warsaw. The Red Army finally crossed the Vistula River on 17 January 1945 to 'liberate' the ruins in a matter of hours, meeting little resistance from the demoralised Nazi troops.

... and this is 'Exodus'

Museum of the Warsaw Uprising

The full narrative of the uprising is related in detail at a museum which opened on 1 August 2004 to mark the 60th anniversary. It is situated to the west of the city centre and is easily reached by tram and bus. Though somewhat confusing in its layout (perhaps intentionally), the museum documents the 63 days of the uprising using period weapons, photographs, posters, films, uniforms and mock-ups of sewers and bunkers. A film in English is shown daily at midday.

ul. Grzybowska 79. Tel: 022 539 79 05. www.1944.pl. Open: Mon, Wed & Fri 8am–6pm, Thur 8am–8pm, Sat & Sun 10am–6pm. Bus: 151, 155, 100; Tram: 1, 22, 24, 32. Admission charge. Free on Sun.

Inner courtyard at Warsaw University Library

which can be climbed for the best views of the Old Town and the Vistula River. Continuing southwards you come to the **Adam Mickiewicz Monument**, dating from 1889. Behind that rises the **Carmelite Church** from the 17th century. Next door stands the majestic **Radziwiłł Palace** (Presidential Palace), a building that has witnessed many important events in Poland's history. The 1791 constitution was passed here, the Warsaw Pact signed in 1955, and the Round Table talks in 1989 between the communists, the Catholic Church and the opposition took place within its walls. Since 1995, it has been the president's residence, hence the tight security. The **Warsaw University Campus** (Uniwersytet Warszawaski) is 200m (220yds) further along, with the Baroque student **Church of the Holy Cross** across the road. A statue of a pensive Nicolaus Copernicus sits a little way to the south of the campus.

Łazienki Park

At the opposite end of the Royal Way from the Old Town lies peaceful Łazienki Park, the perfect antidote to Warsaw's fumes and concrete. The area was a hunting reserve until the 1760s when Poland's last monarch, King Stanisław August Poniatowski, transformed it into an English park. He later added the palace on the lake, which incorporated the existing bathhouse (*Łazienki* in Polish, hence the park's name). The Nazis tried to blow the palace up but only caused limited damage. Take a guided tour to see the interior, including the royal bathhouse and the ballroom.

Łazienki Park is a much-loved place for Varsovians to come for their traditional Sunday-afternoon stroll or to attend free Chopin concerts, which are held every Sunday at the Art Deco Chopin monument dating from 1926. In summer, if you are very lucky, you may catch a performance at the Island Amphitheatre, which dates from 1790. Peacocks and other fauna roam the lawns at will, many species of tree provide welcome shade, and the park is a place to unwind and rest aching feet after a few days' sightseeing.

Palace. ul. Agrykola 1. Tel: 022 621 62 41. www.lazienki-krolewskie.pl. Open: Tue–Sun 8am–3.30pm. Bus: 100, 138, 151, 182, 187, 188.

Palace of Culture and Science

Even after more than 50 years, the Palace of Culture and Science is still Poland's highest building. Built between 1952 and 1955, this monolithic piece of Stalinist architecture measures 231m (758ft) (making it Europe's fifth-tallest

A rare red squirrel in Łazienki Park

The imposing Palace of Culture and Science

JEWISH WARSAW

Exploring the Jewish sights of Warsaw can be an exhausting undertaking on foot, as the various monuments and places of interest are spread out over a wide area in the districts of Muranów and Mirów. This gives an indication of the size of the Jewish ghetto and the community that disappeared during World War II, never to return.

The best place to start a tour is in the north on Stawki Street where you will find the **Umschlagplatz**, where transports left with their human cargoes to go to the death camp at Treblinka. Between 1940 and 1943, more than 300,000 of Warsaw's Jews departed from here to their deaths. The spot is now marked by an unremarkable and crumbling marble monument. If you fancy a long walk, Warsaw's huge **Jewish cemetery** is 15 minutes to the southwest. Having survived the war years virtually unscathed, this cemetery has the biggest number of Jewish gravestones in Europe (150,000), and is still in use. Back on Stawki Street, walk south to **Willy Brandt Square**. In this park, the German chancellor fell to his knees during a visit in 1970 in an act of penitence for the crimes his nation had committed here. The peaceful stretch of grass is home to the **Monument to the Heroes of the Ghetto**, another powerful piece of socialist realism made from granite, which the Nazis had intended to use for their victory monument. Directly to the south is the **Pawiak Prison Museum**, the Gestapo's main jail where around 37,000 prisoners were executed. From here, take any tram south to the large roundabout where Jana Pawła II meets Świętkrzyska, then walk northeast to see the neo-Romanesque **Nożyk Synagogue** which miraculously survived World War II, and nearby **Próżna Street**, an eerie section of the ghetto that survived the end of the war. The buildings are still pockmarked with bullet holes. A piece of the wall that surrounded the ghetto can be seen between No 55 Sienna Street and No 62 Złota Street, and there is another fragment in Walicòw Street.

Nożyk Synagogue

building) and has over 3,000 rooms. The palace was a gift of friendship from the Soviet Union and is an ever-present and dominating reminder on the capital's skyline of the years Poland spent under communist rule. It remains controversial to this day, and many Varsovians hate the sight of it.

Inside, you will find a mammoth congress hall that has echoed to both the ranting of communist congress delegates and to rock music concerts. Above that extends a kind of self-contained vertical town with a post office, cinemas, museums, three theatres and a library. Some 14 super-speed lifts whisk visitors up in several eardrum-warping seconds to the main attraction for tourists, the viewing platform at 114m (374ft). The views are superb but, unfortunately, due to Warsaw's unbridled building boom, they are becoming obscured by a ring of glass and steel monstrosities under construction nearby.

Plac Defilad 1. Tel: 022 656 6134. www.pkin.pl

Praga

The under-visited district of Praga across the Vistula River from the Old Town was not destroyed during World War II, and it has kept a hint of the city's pre-war atmosphere. Lower rents and the distinctive character of the area have attracted artists to take up residence here in the last decade, and the new inhabitants have created a little bohemian quarter all for themselves.

There are a number of specific sights worth crossing the Vistula River to see. The neo-Gothic **Cathedral of the Archangel Michael** towers over Praski Park by the Śląsko-Dąbrowski Bridge leading from the Old Town. It was built at the end of the 19th century but was blasted to dust in World War II. The rebuilt cathedral is most impressive when illuminated after dark.

A short way along Al. Solidarności stands the pretty **Orthodox Church of St Mary Magdalene**, another 19th-century structure with typical squat onion domes and a Byzantine layout. The church is now the centre of the Orthodox Church in Poland.

Perhaps the greatest draw in Praga is the **Russian Market** held in the

The Orthodox Church of St Mary Magdalene

The grand interior of Wilanów Palace

unpronounceable and unused Dziesięciolecia Stadium near the Poniatowski Bridge. It's a huge bazaar selling everything from Vietnamese clothing to spare parts for Polish Fiats. Watch out for pickpockets.

Wilanów

Some 6km (4 miles) south of Łazienki Park you will find another palace surrounded by a park, the erstwhile summer residence of King Jan Sobieski III. The name comes from the Italian 'Villa Nuova', as it was built in the Italian Baroque style. The grand rooms of the palace, which are filled with period furniture and artwork, can be visited on a guided tour. Around the palace extend numerous parks and gardens in a variety of styles. There's also a poster museum and an 18th-century Orangery housing an art gallery.

Wilanów Palace. ul. S. K. Potockiego 10/16. Tel: 022 842 81 01. www.wilanow-palac.art.pl. Open: mid-Sept–Apr Mon, Wed–Sat 9.30am–4pm, Sun 10.30am–4.30pm; May–mid-Sept Mon, Wed & Sat 9.30am–6.30pm, Tue, Thur & Fri 9.30am–4.30pm, Sun 10.30am–6.30pm. Last admission 1 hour before closing. Admission charge. Free on Sat. Bus: 180 or 116 from Krakowskie Przedmieście.

The northeast

The northeast of the country, which borders on the Russian enclave of Kaliningrad, Lithuania and Belarus, includes the historical territories of Warmia and Masuria in the north and Mazovia and Podlasie further south. Although the region contains the capital, Warsaw, most of its expanse is tranquil countryside speckled with literally hundreds of lakes. The most celebrated of Poland's protected areas, the Białowieża National Park, can be found in Podlasie.

Warmia and Masuria

Warmia and Masuria are two historical regions, although today they run seamlessly into one another. They possess the most lakes in Poland, and it is this feature that defines the region from a tourist's point of view. With so

much water sloshing around, it is no surprise that watersports are big in this part of the country. The Great Masurian Lake District is the top place to head for as it has Poland's largest inland body of water, Lake Śniardwy (114sq km/71 square miles). Another famous stretch of water is the Elbląg-Ostróda Canal, remarkable for its unique system of slipways that sees boats making up almost 100m (330ft) difference in water levels by being hauled across land on rails. Away from the water, the region has much to keep landlubbers occupied. The town of Olsztyn and the nearby Olsztynek Museum of Folk Architecture, one of the region's highlights, provide a couple of days' entertainment, as does the former capital of the Warmian bishopric, Lidzbark Warmiński.

Mazovia and Podlasie

Unlike Warmia and Masuria, these two historical provinces are relatively distinct from one another. Mazovia is

Warsaw's hinterland, a place of castles, palaces and undulating agricultural land stretching from Poland's unremarkable second city, Łódź, to the area east of the Vistula River. It is dominated by the urban sprawl of Warsaw, with its almost 2 million inhabitants, but you don't have to travel far from the capital to find peaceful, rural scenes in stark contrast to the bustling city. Apart from Warsaw and Łódź, Mazovia possesses several fascinating historical towns such as Płock and Łowicz. It is also where you will find a place with a more infamous name – Treblinka – the second-largest Nazi concentration camp after Oświęcim (Auschwitz).

The further east you travel into Podlasie, the more traditionally rural the scene becomes, with tiny villages, timber houses, wooded plains and increasingly poor roads. This is one of only a handful of places in the country where different ethnicities mix, and you are certain to notice Lithuanian, Belarusian and Ukrainian influences. There is even a small Tatar community who have their own wooden mosques in the villages of Kruszyniany and Bohoniki. The unrivalled highlight of Podlasie is the Białowieża National Park, which straddles the border with Belarus, but the whole region is an excellent place to enjoy the great outdoors in any season of the year. It's ideal for a spot of birdwatching, mushroom picking or just for a

Statue of Nicolaus Copernicus in Olsztyn

stroll through the forests without meeting a soul. The biggest town is Białystok in the northeast, but urban settlements are pretty thin on the ground.

Lidzbark Warmiński

Some 46km (28 miles) north of Olsztyn stands one of the red-brick fortresses so typical of northern Poland. It is one of the greatest pieces of architecture in Warmia and a must-see on all itineraries in the northeast. The town was the capital of the Warmian bishopric for four centuries, but you would hardly know it today as much was destroyed in World War II. The castle is the reason for coming here, and with its hefty turrets guarding each corner and huge Gothic arched windows, it is a truly impressive sight. The riverside building dates from the late 14th century, and was used as the bishop's palace for four centuries. When the bishops left, it fell into disrepair and was used as a barracks and an orphanage, among other things. Renovation began in the 1920s, and luckily the castle survived World War II unscathed. Much of the interior now holds the regional museum.

pl. Zamkowy 1. Tel: 089 767 2111. Museum open: May–Sept Tue–Sun 9am–5pm; Oct–Apr Tue–Sun 10am–4pm. Bus: hourly to and from Olsztyn.

Olsztyn

Originally a Polish town, the partition of Poland in the late 18th century saw Olsztyn come under Prussia, and this remained the situation until after World War II, during which 40 per cent of the town was destroyed. Though not the prettiest of Poland's cities, when visiting the Great Masurian Lakes, Olsztyn is the most convenient place to reach from almost anywhere in the

The warm red brick of Lidzbark Warmiński

A traditional windmill at the *skansen* in Olsztynek

country, and it is by far the biggest settlement around. It is also easy to get to the Olsztynek *skansen* to the south from here.

Olsztyn has a compact Old Town where most of the sights are grouped. In the middle of the market square you will find the town hall and around it the Gothic High Gate, a cathedral and a 14th-century castle housing a museum and quarters that once belonged to Nicolaus Copernicus. The cathedral's towers dominate the skyline, and its interior is one of the best in the northeast.

Olsztynek

One of the folk highlights of the northeast is the *skansen* or open-air museum at Olsztynek, 26km (16 miles) south of Olsztyn. The museum is northeast of the village and contains 40 timber structures from Warmia and Masuria, as well as some traditional Lithuanian dwellings. There is also an 18th-century Protestant church, a couple of windmills and many other workshops and agricultural buildings. Visitors can enter many of the houses which have period interiors complete with furniture and other folksy regalia.
ul. Sportowa 21.
Tel: 089 519 2164.
www.olsztynek.com.pl/skansen.
Open: Apr & Oct Tue–Sun 9am–3pm,
May–Aug Tue–Sun 9am–5pm,
Sept Tue–Sun 9am–4pm.

Kanal Ostródzko-Elbląski (The Elbląg-Ostróda Canal)

The Kanal Ostródzko-Elbląski (Elbląg-Ostróda Canal) is an 81km (50-mile) long stretch of man-made waterway, linking the towns of Elbląg in the north, a few kilometres short of the Gulf of Gdańsk, and Ostróda in the south. Although it links two unremarkable towns, a pleasure cruise along the canal is an interesting and relaxing experience. The route is a mix of canal and lake, but the main features are the slipways used to overcome the 100m (330ft) difference in water levels between the two towns. Boats are put on rails and simply dragged across dry land to the next bit of water.

The canal was built by Dutch engineer Georg Jakob Steenke in the mid-19th century as part of efforts to improve the region's infrastructure. It was created primarily to transport timber from the Iława Lake Region to the Baltic Sea, and took 30 years to build due to the technical obstacles the Prussian

An ingenious method of overcoming a hill!

engineers had to overcome. Steenke devised a clever system of locks on the canal, but it is the slipways that are the real touch of genius, and nowhere else in Europe will you find such an arrangement. The slipways are situated on a 10km (6-mile) stretch on the northern section of the canal. Huge carriages transport boats along sections of rail and set them down again in the water on the other side. It is an ingenious and unique method of travelling by boat over dry land and of overcoming the height difference on the canal. Tourist cruises began in the 1930s and, despite the Red Army damaging the locks and slipways at the end of World War II, sailings restarted in 1948 and have been running ever since. Of course, pleasure boats are now the only craft you will find on the canal.

Day trips run on the canal from May until September, with boats taking 11 hours to complete the journey. Needless to say, the boats set off in both directions early in the morning and arrive in the evening at the other end. There is limited food and drink on board, so bring a packed lunch. A pair of binoculars is also a good idea as the route takes the boats through a nature reserve (Drużno Lake), home to many species of bird.

The canal cuts through peaceful woodland

Practical information

If you intend to travel the whole route from Elbląg to Ostróda, or vice versa, you will in all likelihood need to stay the night in both places. The recommended place to stay in Ostróda is the Hotel Promenada (*tel: 089 646 81 00*), and in Elbląg the Hotel Viwaldi (*tel: 055 236 25 42*) is a decent option. Elbląg is easy to reach by train from Gdańsk. To get to Ostróda, take a train from Warsaw or Gdańsk and change at Iława.

The **Żegluga Ostródzko-Elbląska** company operates cruises on the canal (*www.zegluga.com.pl*). A minimum of 20 passengers is required for the sailing to take place, and the boats can carry a maximum of 65 people.

Wilczy Szaniec (The Wolf's Lair)

Anyone interested in World War II history should not pass up a trip to the Wolf's Lair, around 50km (31 miles) northeast of Olsztyn near the village of Gierłoż. Many assume that Hitler spent the war in Berlin, but apart from a four-month stint in Ukraine, from June 1941 until November 1944 Hitler stayed in a complex of bunkers in this corner of Poland because it was one of the few places where he felt safe. Ironically, this is where he was almost assassinated by the bomb of Colonel Claus von Stauffenberg. It's a large set of ruins now, but a popular one with guided tours.

Gierłoż. Tel: 089 752 4429.
www.wolfsschanze.home.pl

Masurian Lake District

Spread between the towns of Olsztyn in the west and Suwałki in the east, the Masurian Lake District is an area of thick woodland, still, misty lakes and several bustling resorts. This is one of Poland's most attractive tourist areas and the ideal spot for a week on the water. There are thousands of lakes interlinked by rivers and canals that, in some places, are wide and deep enough to allow ferries to pass between towns. Boat trips, canoeing, waterskiing, angling and plain old swimming are all popular activities, especially in the summer months, and some of the lakes freeze over in winter creating superb conditions for skating. With so much water around, it is no surprise that this is a habitat for hundreds of species of wildfowl and other animals and insects. Lake Łuknajno, near the town of Mikołajki, is a UNESCO Biosphere Reserve and home to a colony of mute swans, one of the last remaining in Europe.

The two biggest lakes are **Lake Śniardwy** and **Lake Mamry**. Śniardwy

Dense forest is found throughout the Masurian Lake District

The water and reeds of the Masurian Lakes are home to many species of wildlife.

is the largest inland expanse of water in Poland at 110sq km (68 square miles). Niegocin, Tałty, Nidzkie, Laśmiady and Ros are other large lakes in the area. The most popular resorts to head for are **Giżycko** and **Mikołajki** (*see p46*), though in summer these can be uncomfortably crowded, and accommodation is hard to come by. The further east you head, the less crowded things usually become, even in the height of summer.

In addition to the ferries that operate between Giżycko, Mikołajki and a few smaller towns, the area is well served by rail.

Giżycko

The small town of Giżycko, which, like Mikołajki 40km (25 miles) to the south, straddles two lakes (Niegocin and Mamry), lacks charm and has only a couple of places worth seeing. Most of the town's buildings were destroyed in World War II and in the post-war years replaced with many typical communist-era recreational blocks. Apart from the lakes themselves, Giżycko's attractive waterfront and a Prussian-era star-shaped fortress to the west are the town's chief attractions.

Mikołajki

The lakeside town of Mikołajki is often described as the Venice of Masuria thanks to its watery location at the meeting point of two lakes. While perhaps not quite living up to this grand description, Mikołajki is possibly the best resort in the region. The downside is that crowds pack the streets in summer and accommodation is hopelessly booked up.

The main draw is the waterfront, where you will find a marina lined with outdoor bars and cafés, and boats of all shapes and sizes bobbing in the water, as well as the jetty from which the ferries leave, and a small beach area. The town itself has a low-rise main square, and the finest piece of architecture is the 19th-century Protestant Church of the Holy Trinity by Lake Tałty. The UNESCO Biosphere Reserve can be found 4km (2½ miles) to the east. A tower provides bird-watchers with the best views of the lake and its feathered inhabitants.

Święta Lipka

Święta Lipka is one of Poland's finest Baroque churches situated almost in the middle of nowhere, just to the north of Lake Dejnowa and 25km (15½ miles) southwest of the town of Kętrzyn. Its name means 'Holy Lime Tree', and the legend about a tree of this kind led to a church of such grandeur being built in this remote location. The story goes that a Prussian prisoner in nearby Kętrzyn received a visitation from the Virgin Mary shortly before he was due to be executed. She gave him a tree trunk, out of which he carved a statue of the Virgin. Next morning, when the judges saw the beauty he had created, they interpreted it as a sign from heaven and released the man, who placed the statue in a lime tree. This became a shrine with curative powers. Shut down and destroyed in 1526 by the Teutonic Knights after their conversion to Lutheranism, the site was bought by Catholic Poles in 1620.

Święta Lipka

The Baroque organ at Święta Lipka

The Jesuits built the church we see today, employing Vilnius architect Jerzy Ertly to carry out the work.

The highlights of the church are the incredible trompe l'oeil ceiling frescoes by Maciej Mayer, the Baroque organ containing 5,000 pipes fashioned by Johann Mozengel, and the altar incorporating a reproduction of the original lime tree, atop of which stands a statue of the Virgin Mary. This is one of the most popular sites on Poland's Marian pilgrimage circuit, and a place where foreign visitors can stand back in awe at unfeigned Polish religious fervour. Expect enormous crowds on special occasions, especially in August. There are organ recitals every Friday evening in summer.

Bus: from Olsztyn, Lidzbark Warmiński and Kętrzyn.

The Suwałki region

The area around the town of Suwałki, in the far northeast near the border with Lithuania, is one of the least-visited parts of Poland and the ideal place to escape mass tourism. To the east of Suwałki and Augustów lies an area of virtually uninhabited woodland interspersed with small lakes, extending east into Belarus. Pre-war

Suwałki was an ethnically mixed place with Jews, Poles, Lithuanians, Tatars and Belarusians living peacefully side by side. The Jews have gone, leaving behind just an empty cemetery, but some of the diversity remains. This is best seen in the town's architecture, churches and cemeteries. Otherwise, Suwałki is a drowsy provincial town, but interesting for its remote ambience.

Around Suwałki there are several other interesting and attractive spots. Some 11km (7 miles) southeast of the town is the small **Wigry National Park** centred on Lake Wigry where the local beaver colony is the main draw. Some **Jacwingian burial mounds** can be found 4km (2½ miles) north of the town, near the village of Szwajcaria. The Jacwingians were a tribe of people related to Lithuanians who occupied this region between the 3rd and 5th centuries AD. Some 31km (19 miles) south is the town of **Augustów**, an excellent gateway to the area of forests and lakes to the east.

Białystok

The eastern city of Białystok does not feature heavily on many tourists' itineraries and remains somewhat off the beaten track. However, this city of almost 300,000 is worth a visit if you happen to be in the area for the examples of traditional wooden architecture that have somehow survived, and for the unique mix of Polish and Belarusian culture that you

Windmill near Białystok

won't see anywhere else in the country. You may also find yourself in Białystok on your way to the Wooden Tatar mosques at Kruszyniany and Bohoniki. Otherwise, World War II put paid to any aesthetic beauty the city had and also witnessed the disappearance of its large Jewish community. The cathedral, former Jewish ghetto, Branicki Palace and Jewish cemetery to the northeast constitute the city's main sights. Białystok's most famous son was one Ludvik Zamenhof (1859–1917), the inventor of Esperanto.

Wooden Tatar mosques at Kruszyniany and Bohoniki

It may come as a surprise to many that there are mosques on the Polish border with Belarus, but the story of how there came to be a Muslim Tatar community in this unlikely setting explains all. In the 13th century, Genghis Khan united the tribes of Central Asia who then rode east, plundering the towns, cities and villages that they found on their way. One of these tribes was a particularly ferocious bunch, the Tatars. Soon they reached Europe, getting as far as Vienna and Kraków, but later withdrew to central Russia, south Ukraine and Crimea. Crimean Tatars were drafted into the Lithuanian army in the 15th century and began to settle in the area. In the 17th century, King

Jan Sobieski rewarded the Tatars, who had helped him defeat the Turks at the battle of Vienna, with land in what is now the border area between Poland and Belarus. Many of these communities still exist today, predominantly on the Belarusian side of the border.

The villages of Kruszyniany and Bohoniki, 37km (23 miles) apart and both pressed against the border, are two of these settlements on the Polish side. Their star attractions are two modest timber mosques that can be visited. Both buildings will be locked when you arrive and you should ask

(*cont on p52*)

Branicki Palace, one of the central attractions in Białystok

Białowieża National Park

The Białowieża Forest, which straddles the border dividing Poland from Belarus, represents the last remaining fragment of the immense forest that once covered the plains of Europe. Only a few sections were declared a national park in 1921, and a campaign to do the same with the whole Białowieża Forest is ongoing. Within the park there are 'Strict Reserves' which can only be visited as part of a guided tour. The rest of the park and forest can be wandered at will.

Over 11,000 species inhabit the forest, though most visitors come to catch a glimpse of just one, the European bison. This can be seen in a special reserve where captive animals are kept, but many others (around 300) roam free in the surrounding woodland. Bison were once found all over the continent but were slowly forced east by deforestation. By the end of World War I, they had disappeared from here, their last refuge. Luckily, some 50 specimens were kept in zoos, and it was by breeding these animals that a population was reinstated in Białowieża. Today, bison are exported from here to zoos around the world. Other interesting and rare animals, for which the forest provides a safe

Wild boar in the national park

Białowieża Forest

can follow. The bison reserve is located around 4km (2½ miles) to the west of Białowieża on the road to Hajnówka. Other places that can be visited without a forest guide include the Royal Oaks Way, a group of huge 400-year-old oaks, the Forest Museum and the Palace Park.

The Białowieża area is beautiful at any time of year, but autumn, when the leaves turn a million shades of red, orange and yellow, and winter, when snow lies on the ground, are particularly attractive. There are also fewer visitors at these times of year, which intensifies the primeval deep-forest atmosphere.

haven, include lynx, boar, wolves, beavers and various kinds of bat, rodent, newt and frog. The 10,501ha (25,948 acres) which make up the Białowieża National Park were declared a UNESCO World Natural Heritage Site in 1979.

Most start their visit in the village of Białowieża where it is easy to join a guided tour. To visit the protected areas you must have a guide and enter with a group. You can also enter the forest in a horse-drawn cart, although only a limited number of these are allowed in each day. In addition, there are various marked hiking and cycling paths that visitors

Practical information

One hundred thousand tourists visit the Polish part of the forest annually, many on tour buses. If you do not have your own set of wheels and you are not on a coach trip, getting there is relatively easy. From Warsaw there are rail services to Hajnówka with a change in Siedlce. From Białystok there are direct buses to Białowieża village, or you can travel by rail with a change in Czeremcha. There is adequate accommodation in both Hajnówka and Białowieża, but booking ahead in summer is advisable.

Białowieża National Park.
Tel: 085 682 9700. www.bpn.com.pl

The imposing cathedral in Łowicz

around for someone to open up and show you the interior. Kruszyniany's mosque dates from the 18th century and is still a functioning place of worship, with services taking place once a month (there are no Friday prayers). The smaller, green mosque in Bohoniki was built in the mid-19th century. The mosques naturally receive many visitors from the Arab world. Both villages have Muslim cemeteries, and Kruszyniany has a wonderful yurt (Central Asian nomad's tent) restaurant that serves traditional Tatar food, an excellent place to finish your day. Neither village has any accommodation, and visitors almost always return to Białystok at the end of the day. There is little public transport to or from either place, and

connections are difficult. The best way to make the journey is in your own car, and many people hire a taxi for the day in Białystok, 50km (31 miles) to the west.

Łowicz

The main draw in Łowicz (pronounced *woveech*), 150km (93 miles) west of Warsaw, is its colossal cathedral on the old marketplace. Dating from the Gothic era, almost every style since can be seen inside and out. Twelve archbishops of Gniezno are buried inside. Across the square there is a museum housing a collection of regional folk items. Łowicz is a centre for folk culture in the region, which is best seen during the Corpus Christi celebrations in late May or early June.

Around Łowicz

Arkadia

Arkadia is a romantic park, around 5km (3 miles) west of Nieborów, created by Princess Helena Radziwiłł in the 1770s and dotted with follies and lakes. Many of the pieces of art that once graced the parkland were collected by the princess on her travels around Europe. When she died, they were taken to Nieborów, and the buildings fell into disrepair. Almost untouched since the late 18th century, the ruins of the follies and the overgrown pathways lend the place a uniquely romantic atmosphere, and create the ideal location for a relaxing stroll.
Open: 10am–dusk daily.

Oporów

The tiny village of Oporów possesses a fine Gothic castle, one of only a handful to have survived to this day in its original state. Lying 35km (22 miles) to the northwest of Łowicz, it was built in the 15th century for the archbishop of Gniezno and has changed very little since. The building underwent extensive restoration after World War II and since then has been a museum. The castle is surrounded by a moat and parkland.
Tel: 024 285 9122.
www.zamekoporow.pl. Open: Tue–Sun 10am–4pm. Difficult to reach by public transport. Train from Łowicz to Żychlin, then bus or taxi.

The northeast

Ruined folly, Arkadia

Palace of Nieborów, now a museum

Palace of Nieborów

Designed by the Dutchman Tylman of Gameren (responsible for much of Warsaw's original architecture) in the late 17th century, the perfectly symmetrical Palace of Nieborów can be found 15km (9 miles) southeast of Łowicz. Originally built for the archbishop of Gniezno, Cardinal Radziejowski, it was owned for much of its history, up until World War II, by the well-known Radziwiłł family. Now in state ownership, the interiors are a museum full of period furnishings and hundreds of priceless works of art. This is one of Poland's best-kept palaces, and it is surrounded by equally well-pruned gardens. The French Garden on the southern side

of the palace is dotted with pieces of sculpture brought here from nearby Arkadia (*see p55*). To the west is a less formal English-style park.

Nieborów 232.
Tel: 046 838 56 35.
www.nieborow.art.pl.
Open: Mar & Apr Tue–Sun 10am–4pm;
May & June Mon–Sun 10am–6pm;
July–Sept Mon–Fri 10am–4pm, Sat &
Sun 10am–6pm; Oct Tue–Sun
10am–3.30pm. Tours are self-guided.
Admission charge.

Sromów Folk Museum

Another place of interest in the immediate surroundings of Łowicz, this time a few kilometres to the north, is the privately owned folk museum in the tiny rural hamlet of Sromów. This is the life's work of folk artist and avid collector Julian Brzozowski, who lives in the village. He was compelled to create the museum when his house became too small to house all his collections. Two of the four buildings house mechanical scenes of traditional village life with beautifully carved figures dressed in traditional costume. The other two contain old carriages and regional folk items such as pieces of furniture, handicrafts, costumes and artwork. If you are very lucky, Mr Brzozowski,

now 83 years of age, will show you around himself.

Open: Mon–Sat 9am–7pm, Sun noon–7pm.

Płock

The clifftop town of Płock (pronounced *pwotsk*), 115km (71 miles) west of Warsaw, has a fine historical centre overlooking the Vistula River, the highlight of which is the huge cathedral originally dating from the 12th century. This was the seat of the Polish kings in the 11th century and a major bishopric. One of

A Nativity scene at Sromów Folk Museum

The rooftops of Pułtusk

the most attractive features of the cathedral is its bronze doors. These are copies of a set of doors which were taken to Novgorod in Russia and only rediscovered 600 years later in the 1970s. The two towers called Zegarowa and Szlachecka next to the cathedral are all that remains of the royal castle. The **Mazovian Museum** near the cathedral has a fine collection of Art Nouveau items.

Mazovian Museum. Ulica Tumska 8. Tel: 024 364 70 71. www. muzeumplock.art.pl. Open: Tue–Sun 10am–5pm. Admission charge.

Pułtusk

A common day-trip destination from Warsaw 60km (37 miles) to the south, Pułtusk is an interesting town with a surprisingly lively history. It is one of Mazovia's oldest settlements and served as the residence of the Płock bishops in the 15th and 16th centuries. Decline set in after several fires and the marauding Swedes inflicted much damage. In 1806, Napoleon defeated the Russians here in a major battle, but the Russians were back in 1944 to rid the town of the Nazis, destroying 80 per cent of it in the process. In 1868, Pułtusk was even hit by a meteorite, bits of which are exhibited in the British Museum in London.

Rebuilt and now on the tourist circuit, Pułtusk has a long, attractive market square, dominated by the town hall in the middle. The red-brick Gothic tower houses the **Regional Museum**. To the north is the Gothic

Collegiate Church, refashioned in the Renaissance style in the 16th century. To the south stands the castle where the bishops once resided. Napoleon stayed here twice in 1806 and again in 1812. It is now a hotel and conference centre.
Regional Museum. Ryneki.
Tel: 023 692 5132.
Open: Tue–Sun 10am–4pm.

Treblinka

Some 80km (50 miles) northeast of Warsaw is the site of the Nazis' second-largest death camp after Oświęcim (Auschwitz). Following an uprising by camp inmates in the summer of 1943, Treblinka was razed to the ground. A granite monument was erected in a clearing in the forest here after the war and is surrounded by 17,000 standing stones bearing the names of towns and villages. This is the grave of 800,000 people, mostly Jews, who died here in the gas chambers and were then cremated. Nothing remains of the original camp (unlike at Auschwitz), but the place is no less powerful.
Difficult to reach by public transport. Train from Warsaw to village of Małkinia, then taxi.

These simple words say it all

Małopolska and the Carpathian Mountains

Małopolska translates as 'Lesser Poland', but it is actually larger than Wielkopolska ('Great Poland') on the other side of the country. The presence of Kraków and the Tatra Mountains makes this one of the most interesting and popular tourist regions of Poland.

Kraków (or Cracow) is Poland's premier tourist attraction, and just a few minutes in Poland's third-largest city are sufficient to see why. Nowhere else in the country did such a fine historical centre survive World War II so intact, and Kraków's wealth of historical buildings from every period almost rivals the wonders of Prague. The problem can be that very few tourists go beyond the city limits (except perhaps to visit the salt mines at Wieliczka), and so the rest of Małopolska to the east remains relatively off the beaten track. Those who do venture into this corner of

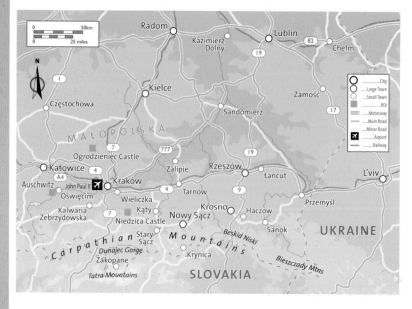

Poland will be richly rewarded. This is one of Poland's least inhabited regions, and if you want to get away from the stresses of modern life, a journey to the rural areas of Małopolska is like travelling back in time. The area also has some exquisite historical settlements, the best of which must be UNESCO-listed Zamość, a perfectly preserved Renaissance town, Kazimierz Dolny, and Sandomierz. Apart from Kraków to the west, Rzeszów and Lublin are the only major urban centres in the east and serve as major transport hubs for the region.

The flip side to Małopolska is its mountain areas that rise on its southern flanks. The Tatras, Pieniny, Beskid Niski and the Bieszczady Mountains are all part of the Carpathian range that arcs from western Slovakia to central Romania, and forms a natural border between Poland and Slovakia. The Tatras are the highest and most dramatic and enjoy some of the best snow conditions in the region, making this the ideal place for skiing and snowboarding. The town of Zakopane is the gateway to the Tatras and a major winter resort. In summer, the mountains are crisscrossed with well-marked hiking trails and mountain-biking routes. The nearby Pieniny and Podhale areas are home to an ethnic minority called the Górale (or Highlanders) who have a distinct culture and language that they are

Snowy Częstochowa

trying to keep alive. The Bieszczady, in the far southeastern corner, is a remote mountain region where bears and wolves still live in the wild.

Wooden churches are a striking feature across southern Poland. Some of the best examples can be found in Małopolska, with the biggest Gothic timber church in the world located in Haczów. The largest *skansen* (open-air museum) is located in the town of Sanok. Częstochowa, to the northwest of Kraków, is Poland's most important place of pilgrimage and is famous for the legendary *Black Madonna*.

KRAKÓW

Kraków, Poland's third-largest city, is by far the country's most popular tourist destination. Left virtually untouched by World War II, the city has a historical centre with buildings ranging from Romanesque to Baroque. The uniqueness of the small central core, whose only rival in the region is Prague, led to a UNESCO listing as early as 1978.

As a major tourist magnet, Kraków has a year-round tourist season, with summer witnessing the biggest crowds. Despite the hordes of visitors that descend on the city, the centre still possesses a magical atmosphere.

History

Kraków's position on several major transcontinental trade routes meant that by the 11th century it had become a large market town. Poland's first rulers made it the seat of a bishopric and then the capital in 1038. Kraków was left in ruins by the Tatars in 1241, but the city was rebuilt with the grid layout that you can see today centred on the main square. King Kazimierz Wielki developed Kraków further in the 14th century when he founded the second university in central Europe, and rebuilt large parts of the city. It was at this time that Jews first came to settle in Kraków.

Kraków's fortunes began to wane in 1596 when King Sigmund Waza III moved the capital to Warsaw. Kings were still crowned and buried at Wawel Cathedral, but the court had gone. Occupation by the Swedes from 1655–7 only added to the city's decline. After the partition of Poland, Kraków found itself under Austria, which was never as harsh as Russia or Prussia. Artists, revolutionary politicians (including Lenin), thinkers and writers were attracted to Kraków in the 19th century and the beginning of the 20th. German occupation during World War II saw the Jewish community disappear and many of Kraków's intellectuals arrested.

The subsequent communist period was not good to Kraków, mainly due to pollution from the nearby Nowa Huta steelworks which the Party built in an attempt to break the city's intellectual and religious traditions. In 1978, the then archbishop of Kraków was elected Pope John Paul II.

The Church of St Mary (see p63)

After the fall of communism, the city was given a major overhaul, and many new hotels, restaurants and businesses opened their doors. Tourists began arriving in droves and Kraków found itself on the map of Europe once again.

Orientation

Although a sprawling city of almost 800,000 souls, the historical centre of Kraków is small and compact, and visitors will rarely have to use public transport. The old town is encircled by a ring of parkland called the Planty.

Within this green belt you will find all the city's major sites, with the main square in the centre and Wawel Castle in the south by the Vistula River. On the other side of the Planty, to the east, lies the Kazimierz district, the former Jewish area, where you will find all the city's Jewish sites and several churches. Most of the hotels and restaurants can be found in the city centre, and most people never leave the confines of the Planty or Kazimierz. If you do, you will find communist prefab tower blocks, a contrast to the historical core.

Małopolska and the Carpathian Mountains

The town hall tower in Kraków

Walk: Kraków historical centre

This walk will take you through Kraków's Old Town, from the Barbican in the north to Wawel Castle in the south.

Allow at least 3 hours for this walk.

Start your exploration of Kraków at the Barbican in the north.

1 Barbican

Situated between the road and the Florian Gate, this hefty red-brick gate was added in 1498 to the medieval ring of defensive walls that encircled the city. These walls were demolished in the 19th century.
Open: 10am–6pm.

2 Florian Gate

Immediately behind the Barbican stands the older Florian Gate built in the 14th century.
After passing through the gate, resist the urge to head straight down Floriańska and turn right into Św. Jana Street. The Czartoryski Museum is on the left-hand side.

3 Czartoryski Museum

Kraków's premier art collection is housed here. Over 1,000 pieces of art from ancient Greece and Egypt, as well as paintings by Rembrandt and Leonardo da Vinci, are just some of the highlights.

*ul. Św. Jana 19. Tel: 012 422 55 66.
www.muzeum-czartoryskich.krakow.pl.
Open: Tue, Thur & Sun 10am–3.30pm,
Wed, Fri & Sat 10am–6pm (7pm in
summer); free admission Thur.
Head along Św. Jana Street until you
reach the 40,000sq m (430,400sq ft)
expanse of the main marketplace.*

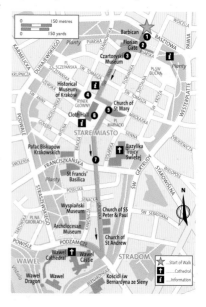

Cloth Hall

4 Rynek Główny

This was medieval Europe's largest square when laid out in the 14th century. Surrounded on all sides by tall town houses in a variety of styles, it creates a grand impression. The Rynek Główny is always a hive of activity, with outdoor cafés hugging the edges, tourists milling around the Cloth Hall, and street performers, open-air exhibitions and strolling locals occupying the cobbles.

The Church of St Mary stands at an angle to the rest of the buildings in the northeastern corner of the square.

5 Church of St Mary

This church is one of Kraków's finest buildings. Built in the latter half of the 14th century, the highlight of the almost overwhelmingly rich interior is the high altar created by Wit Stwosz

between 1477 and 1489. Every hour, day and night, a trumpeter plays the *hejnał* from the top of one of the spires. This seems to stop abruptly in mid-flow as it is said this is when the original trumpeter was struck by a Tatar arrow while warning the city of impending attack in 1241.
Open: Mon–Sat 11.30am–6pm, Sun 2–6pm.
The Cloth Hall dominates the centre of the square.

6 Cloth Hall

On the upper floor of the Renaissance Cloth Hall (Sukiennice) you will find the gallery of 19th-century Polish painting. On the ground floor there is a huge passageway full of craft and souvenir stalls. At the southern end of the Cloth Hall the town hall tower rises 70m (230ft) over the square. This is all that remains of the town hall demolished by the Austrians in 1820.
Leaving the square directly to the south, you find yourself in busy Grodzka Street which leads to the foot of Wawel Hill.

7 Grodzka Street

On the left of Grodzka Street you will see two striking churches, the Baroque Church of SS Peter and Paul with a gallery of statues lining its entrance, and next door the twin towers of the Romanesque Church of St Andrew.
Continue south until you reach the slopes leading up to Wawel Castle and Wawel Cathedral (see pp64–5).

Wawel Hill

The complex of buildings that sits atop Wawel Hill is arguably the most significant place in the country for Poles, as the site is a symbol of the continuity of the Polish state and all it stands for. The castle is one of Europe's finest royal residences, and the cathedral is packed with chapels, tombs and altars in every style going. A visit to the Wawel is the highlight of any visit to Kraków (and perhaps Poland) and should not be missed.

Castle

Having burned down in 1499, the castle was rebuilt in the Renaissance style and, despite the unwanted attentions of the Prussians and Swedes and the meddling of the Austrians who tried to turn it into a barracks, the Renaissance palace has survived almost intact. Every visit to the castle begins on the wonderful arcaded courtyard. From here, visitors embark on the Royal Chambers tour through a door in the southeastern corner. This is a grand series of Renaissance and Baroque rooms complete with period furniture, cassette ceilings and priceless tapestries throughout. The ballroom and the throne room are particularly striking.

The second, less frequent tour takes visitors into the Royal Private Apartments. The rooms, furniture and

The gaggle of buildings on Wawel Hill

The courtyard at Wawel Castle

fittings give an idea of how the monarch and their family would have lived while residing at the Wawel.

Back down on the courtyard, take a look at the Treasury and Armoury in the original Gothic rooms which survived the fire of 1499. The unrivalled highlight is the sword used at every coronation from 1320 onwards. The Museum of Oriental Art, housing 17th-century Turkish weaponry and other items captured at the Battle of Vienna, and the Lost Wawel exhibition, showcasing archaeological finds made on Wawel Hill, can both be accessed from the courtyard.

Cathedral

Wawel Cathedral is to the Poles what Westminster Abbey is to the British or the Cathedral of St Vitus is to the Czechs. It is not only a place of worship and the coronation church of the once great kingdom of Poland, but a national burial site for kings and their families, noteworthy politicians, and celebrated poets and writers. Anyone with even a passing interest in Polish affairs should come to see the final resting place of the people who shaped the history of this nation.

The Gothic building you see today dates from 1364 and is the third church to stand on the site. Inside, you will see

The Gothic cathedral at Wawel

every style to have been in fashion since, created by some of the country's best-known artists. One of the most impressive parts of the cathedral is the amazing Sigmund Chapel in green sandstone and red marble. Many other ornate chapels line the nave, and the interior is packed with the tombs of various kings and bishops. Look out for the tombs of kings Kazimierz Wielki, who did so much for Kraków, and Władysław Jagiełło. Down in the crypt there are the tombs of poet

Adam Mickiewicz, King Jan Sobieski III, the Waza Dynasty, interwar dictator Józef Piłsudski, and 18th-century military genius Tadeusz Kościuszko. The tower can also be climbed to take a look at the Sigmund Bell weighing 11 tonnes, the largest in Poland.

Tel: 012 422 5155. Most sights open from 9am or 10am until 4pm or 5pm. Some sights are free on Mon. Separate tickets needed for all tours and sights. www.wawel.krakow.pl

Kazimierz

The district of Kazimierz, to the southeast of the old quarter, was home to Kraków's 60,000-plus Jewish community until World War II. It was once a separate city with its own town hall and marketplace, and by the end of the 14th century had grown into one of the region's richest municipalities. Today, it is an area of chic dilapidation and Jewish sites, most of which are centred on wide Szeroka Street, which is more like a long square.

The west of Kazimierz was always predominantly Catholic, and here you will find three magnificent churches – the **Skalka Church**, the **Church of St Catherine** and the **Corpus Christi Church**. The main square is called **Plac Wolnica**, and is home to Kazimierz's own Renaissance **Cloth Hall**. This is now an ethnographic museum which possesses one of the largest collections of traditional folk items in Poland. To the east is the Jewish quarter, beginning with the **Isaac's Synagogue**, Kraków's largest, built in 1644. It is now a museum. At the southern end of Szeroka Street you will find the **Old Synagogue**, the oldest in Poland, which now houses the Jewish Museum. To the north there is the **Remuh Synagogue and Cemetery**. The synagogue is still in use as a place of worship, but burials stopped in the cemetery in the 19th century. Both can be visited when services are not taking place.

The **Tempel Synagogue** on Miodowa Street to the northwest was built in the neo-Romanesque style in the mid-19th century. It has some beautiful decoration and stained-glass windows inside. The **New Jewish Cemetery**, still used by the small Jewish community in Kraków, can be found to the northeast. It contains some 9,000 graves.

One of the most atmospheric parts of Kazimierz is the **Plac Nowy** (New Square), bang in the middle of the district. An open-air flea market takes place around the old Jewish slaughterhouse every Sunday, and the square is lined with 19th-century houses that contain small cafés and restaurants.

Old house in the Jewish quarter, Kazimierz

Małopolska and the Carpathian Mountains

Religion in Poland

Poland is without doubt one of Europe's most devout countries, with 95 per cent of the population claiming to be Roman Catholic. Take a stroll around any town on a Sunday and you will see armies of people dressed in their best clothes going to or coming from services. There seems to be a church on every street corner across the land, and nuns, priests and other church dignitaries are a common sight on the country's streets. Churches are rarely empty, and during Mass there's often standing room only. Young and old form the congregation, and if city dwellers try to convince you that young people are turning away from religion, go out into the countryside and you'll witness the reverse. The church is one of the biggest influences in the life of most Poles and inevitably has an effect on the choices they make.

A major figure in this popularity is Pope John Paul II. His role in bringing down the communist government of Poland and Soviet-backed regimes across Europe cannot be overestimated. When he died in 2005, huge crowds filled the streets of every city, and at places associated with his life candles still burn around the clock.

Many may be surprised at how strong the position of the Church was during the communist era. In no other communist country were so many new churches built, children baptised or priests ordained. This was completely unthinkable to the south in Czechoslovakia, for example, where the regime almost stamped out religion altogether. The result is that Poland is the most religious country on the continent; the Czech Republic is the most atheistic.

Worshippers in front of the *Black Madonna*, Jasna Góra (see pp70–72)

Ornate interior at Święta Lipka (*see pp46–7*)

The role of the Catholic Church in Poland since the fall of communism has often been controversial. In many ways, the Church replaced the Communist Party in Poland in the early 1990s, and it was in this period that religious leaders pushed to have tough anti-abortion and religious instruction laws passed. Abortion is still virtually illegal in Poland and religious education is compulsory. The Church's recent influence through the League of Polish Families on the governing coalition also courted controversy. Many in Poland have also begun to grumble that there are too many priests and churches, and that funds could be spent more wisely.

Religion still greatly affects everyday life in Poland. Almost every day there seems to be a Catholic celebration, and major festivals are public holidays as well as an excuse for a party. Pilgrimage sites can be found across the land, and Poles regularly go to church for confession, Mass and simply to pray and meditate.

The 5 per cent of Poles that are not Roman Catholic mostly belong either to the Uniate Church or to the Eastern Orthodox Church. The Uniate Church was created when the Polish Orthodox Church broke with the Russian Orthodox Church, recognised the supremacy of the pope in Rome but kept its orthodox liturgy. Members of the Orthodox Church are very often people who moved into Poland from Ukraine and Belarus, or just found themselves in the country's borders. There is also a minority of Tatar Muslims in the northeast.

Wieliczka Salt Mines

The best day trip out of Kraków must be to the salt mine of Wieliczka, a UNESCO-listed site since 1978, just 15km (9 miles) southeast of the city centre. At 700 years old, this is the oldest working salt mine in the country. Visitors can descend to the three levels of the mine, a labyrinth of incredible chambers, passageways and halls decorated with sculpture crafted entirely out of salt. The mine's principal showpiece is the Chapel of the Blessed Kinga, a large subterranean church built between 1895 and 1927, 135m (443ft) below the surface. There's also a museum with exhibitions on the history of the mine. The mine is still partially in use, and much of Poland's salt still comes from here. Wieliczka is a tour-bus favourite, so expect crowds in summer.

Tel: 012 278 7302. www.kopalnia.pl. Open: 7.30am–7.30pm Apr–Oct, 8am–5pm Nov–Mar. Admission charge. Train from Kraków. Tours (in Polish and English) take around 2 hours. There is a lot of walking involved, and it can be chilly down in the mines.

AROUND KRAKÓW
Częstochowa

The hilltop Monastery of Jasna Góra in the town of Częstochowa was founded in 1382 by Hungarian monks. It would probably go virtually unnoticed by visitors and Poles alike were it not for the fact that this is

Deep inside the Wieliczka Salt Mines

The Chapel of the Miraculous Picture, which houses the *Black Madonna*, at Jasna Góra

The basilica at Jasna Góra

home to a painting called the *Black Madonna* depicting the Virgin Mary with an infant Jesus. It was given to the monks in 1384, but no one knows when exactly it was painted. The image began to perform miracles, the greatest of which was to halt the Swedes at the monastery walls in the 1650s. Actually, the painting was in Silesia at the time, but is nonetheless attributed with stopping the Deluge, as the Swedish invasion is called. Already attracting thousands of pilgrims, the simple image painted in the Byzantine style was crowned Queen of Poland in 1717.

The **Chapel of the Miraculous Picture** is the oldest part of the monastery and the place where the *Black Madonna* is kept. Next door stands a 17th-century Baroque basilica. There are also three museums on the site – the **600th Anniversary Museum** housing paintings, religious objects and offerings including the Nobel Peace Prize awarded to Lech Wałęsa; the **Arsenal** where you will find Turkish weapons used at the Battle of Vienna; and the **Treasury**.

By far the busiest days in Częstochowa are the Feast of the Assumption on 15 August, and six other days throughout the year when Marian pilgrimages and feasts take place. As many as a million pilgrims descend on the town on these occasions, although the monastery is popular year-round with pilgrims and curious tourists alike.
Monastery. ul. O.A. Kordeckiego 2. Tel: 034 377 77 77.
www.jasnagora.pl. Open: 5.30am–9.30pm.
Museums. Open: Apr–Sept 9am–5pm; Oct–Mar 9am–4pm.

Kalwaria Zebrzydowska

The town of Kalwaria Zebrzydowska, some 33km (20 miles) southwest of Kraków, is home to an important pilgrimage site in Poland, second only to Częstochowa (*see pp70–72*).

A church and monastery were commissioned in 1600 by Mikołaj Zebrzydowski from nearby Lanckorona for the Bernardine order as a stand-in for Jerusalem, which had been lost to the Turks. A total of 40 chapels stands in the complex, and the whole site was added to UNESCO's list of World Cultural Heritage Sites in 1999. The huge Basilica of the Virgin contains the chapel of Our Lady of Kalwaria, which is in turn home to a miracle-working picture of the Virgin Mary and Child that the pilgrims flock to see. The painting is one of the country's holiest items and is said to shed tears from time to time. Kalwaria Zebrzydowska heaves with pilgrims at Easter, when Passion Plays are enacted in the grounds, and the day of the Assumption on 15 August. To add to the religious fervour, Pope John Paul II was born in the village of Wadowice, 14km (8 miles) to the west, and used to be a regular visitor to the basilica and monastery.

Ogrodzieniec Castle

Halfway between Kraków and Częstochowa, this is a picturesque hilltop castle ruin. It is one of the most romantic sights in the country and worth the awkward journey to reach it.
Tel: 032 673 2220.
www.zamek-ogrodzieniec.pl.
Open: Apr–Oct 9am–dusk. Train or bus to Zawiercie, then continue by bus.

Małopolska and the Carpathian Mountains

A light covering of snow for Ogrodzieniec Castle

Małopolska and the Carpathian Mountains

THE SOUTHEAST
Kazimierz Dolny

Kazimierz Dolny is a remarkable little town in Poland's southeastern reaches, a picturesque collection of historical buildings spread over two hills overlooking the Vistula River. The core is gathered around the Rynek (main square), lined with low-rise merchants' houses and dominated by the parish church.
Bus: from Lublin.

Lublin

Industrial Lublin is Poland's ninth-largest city and capital of the Lublin Voivodeship. It is a little remote, but does possess an attractive Old Town,

a castle that was used as a prison by the Nazis, and a beautiful Baroque cathedral. The Jewish community (over 40,000 before World War II) left behind a synagogue and two cemeteries. The Majdanek Nazi death camp, 4km (2½ miles) southeast of the city centre, is the site of one of the largest camps in the country.

Sandomierz

The small, pretty town of Sandomierz has a hilltop historical centre overlooking the Vistula River, and several interesting attractions. Having survived World War II intact, the Old Town is centred on the marketplace and dominated by the 14th-century

The Baroque organ in Sandomierz Cathedral

town hall. This now houses a museum on the town's history. Beneath the Old Town there are numerous cellars that were used to store food and drink. These can be explored as part of a 40-minute guided tour. Sandomierz also has its own cathedral built in the mid-14th century but added to extensively over the centuries. A short walk downhill from the cathedral is the 14th-century castle which now houses the Regional Museum. Along Staromiejska Street, west of the castle, rises the 13th-century Romanesque Church of St James, thought to be the first brick church built in Poland.

Zamość

The Renaissance town of Zamość is one of Poland's true architectural gems and more than deserves its listing as a UNESCO World Cultural Heritage Site. The town was conceived by the great 16th-century Polish statesman Jan Zamoyski, and built by Renaissance architect Bernado Morando in just over a decade in the late 16th century. With its bulky fortifications, Zamość held off the Cossacks and the Swedish, and, despite the Nazis' interest in the town, emerged from World War II unscathed.

Zamość's centrepiece is the pure Renaissance Rynek Wielki (Great Marketplace), accommodating the town hall, numerous Renaissance façades and the Zamość Museum. The cathedral can be found to

the southwest of the Rynek. The Renaissance structure was altered in the 19th century but has retained much of its original architecture. The bell tower outside can be climbed, although the views are disappointing. Another striking feature of the town is its beefy town walls, interrupted by several gates. To the west of the Rynek stands the Zamoyski Palace, now regional authority offices.

Half of Zamość's pre-war population was made up of a thriving Jewish community that occupied the area around the Rynek Solny (Salt

The town hall in Sandomierz

Market) to the north of the main Rynek. The only reminder is the synagogue (now a library) in Zamenhofa Street. Zamość is a truly wonderful place to stroll around and should not be missed if you are in this region of Poland.

www.zamosc.pl

Chełm

Chełm (pronounced *khewm*) lies 70km (43 miles) east of Lublin and just 35km (22 miles) short of the border with Ukraine. It rests on an 800m (2,625ft) layer of bedrock chalk, and the principal attraction in town is a system of tunnels hewn out beneath

The palace museum in Łańcut

the medieval centre. This is a former chalk mine that had over 15km (9 miles) of subterranean passageways and halls by the outbreak of World War II. However, the underground spaces undermined the town and were closed in 1965 after a house collapsed due to subsidence. All but 1,800m (5,906ft) of the mine was filled in, and it is this section that remains for visitors to see today. Apart from the chalk tunnels, Chełm has several attractive churches, the finest of which is the Baroque Piarist Church near the entrance to the tunnels.

Chalk Tunnels. Entrance at ul. Lubelska 55a. Tel: 082 565 25 30. Individual tourists admitted at 11am, 1pm & 4pm (additional times in July & Aug). Tours are in Polish and take around 40 minutes.

Łańcut

The palace in the town of Łańcut (pronounced *winetsoot*), 17km (10 miles) east of Rzeszów, is one of the largest noble residences in the country. A castle and palace had stood on the site since the 15th century, but it was one Stanisław Lubormirski who created the building's new Renaissance core. Later neoclassical and neo-Baroque alterations gave the palace the face you see today. The last owner, Count Alfred Potocki, packed up the palace's collections of art and furniture in 1944 and carted them off to Austria before

the Red Army arrived on the estate. Łańcut was then confiscated by the Polish state and made into a museum.

The exquisite interiors can be visited on an hour-long guided tour. The 40 or so rooms open to the public are packed full of priceless works of art and period furniture. Highlights of the tour include the ballroom, which occasionally hosts concerts, and the dining room.

ul. Zamkowa 1. Tel: 017 225 20 08. www.zamek-lancut.pl. Open: summer Mon 11.30am–4pm, Tue–Fri 9am–4pm, Sat & Sun 10am–6pm. Shorter hours at other times of year. Closed Dec & Jan. Admission charge.

Tarnów

The industrial city of Tarnów has a picturesque renovated historical core based on a central marketplace. This is dominated by a Gothic and Renaissance town hall, which is now home to the **Regional Museum** where visitors will find exhibitions of paintings, furniture, glass and ceramics. Just off the marketplace to the northwest is the town's cathedral. It originally dates from the mid-14th century but underwent a neo-Gothic makeover in the late 19th century. The Jewish cemetery to the north of the historical centre is all that remains of the 20,000-strong Jewish community that was wiped out during World War II. The cemetery, which the Nazis did not touch, holds 3,000 graves and is an eerie sight with its leaning, overgrown

The Renaissance grandeur of Krasiczyn Castle

gravestones etched with fading Hebrew inscriptions. Tarnów has a large Romany population, and the local **Ethnographic Museum** showcases this often overlooked ethnic minority with various exhibits from Romany folk culture.

Regional Museum. Rynek 1. Tel: 014 621 21 49. www.muzeum.tarnow.pl. Open: Tue 9am–5pm, Wed–Fri 9am–3pm, Sun 10am–2pm. Ethnographic Museum. ul. Krakowska 10. Tel: 014 622 06 25. Open: as Regional Museum. Admission charge.

Bieszczady Mountains

The Bieszczady range of mountains, the last peaks before the Carpathians arch into Ukraine and on to Romania, is one of the most sparsely populated parts of the country. This is an area of fir and beech interrupted by alpine meadows where native species of bears, wolves and bison are making a comeback. Much of the region is a protected area, although there is unlimited access for visitors. If you can overcome the lack of infrastructure, the area is ideal for light hiking, and if you really want to get away from it all, this is the place to head for. Good bases from which to strike out into the alpine scenery include **Ustrzyki Górne** and **Wetlina**. Before heading out, make sure you have all the necessary equipment with you, and take a reliable map. The Bieszczady are littered with wooden churches and other examples of traditional timber folk architecture.

Krasiczyn

The tiny village of Krasiczyn, to the west of the town of Przemyśl near the border with Ukraine, boasts one of the finest Renaissance castles in Poland. The place makes an interesting stop-over on journeys out of the country, for instance to L'viv (Lvov) on the other side of the border. The architect of this fine structure was an Italian, Galleazzo Appiani. He designed the castle for the Krasicki family at the end of the 16th century, and the building has never been altered since. Many of the features one would expect from a Renaissance piece of architecture are present (arcading, turrets, sgraffito), and the solid, square, snow-white structure is linked to the outside world by an arcaded bridge across a moat. Tours take visitors to three of the four corner towers, the courtyard and a small gallery.

Tel: 016 671 8321. Open: 10am–4pm. Guided tours leave on the hour. Admission charge.

Sanok

The only place of interest in Sanok, a town north of the Bieszczady and

A typical local scene near Sanok

known across Poland for its AutoSan bus factory, is the open-air museum of folk architecture, the biggest in Poland and one of the most celebrated in Europe. The museum (or *skansen*) is located 1.5km (1 mile) north of the town centre and is home to around 120 traditionally constructed buildings from southeast Poland. Every building style employed by all the region's Highlander ethnic groups, such as the Boyks and Łemks, is represented. The buildings you see have been dismantled in the villages where they once stood and brought here to be pieced back together and protected from fire and other damaging elements. There are windmills, churches, whole inns, ordinary cottages and farmhouses. The school and traditional carved beehives are particularly impressive. *ul. Traugutta 3. Tel: 013 463 09 04. www.skansen.sanok.pl. Open: May–Sept 8am–6pm; Oct 8am–4pm; Nov–Mar 8am–2pm; Apr 9am–4pm.*

Zalipie

You will find the village of Zalipie 30km (18 miles) north of Tarnów, famous for its houses that boast traditionally decorated interiors. The best time to visit is after the Corpus Christi 'Painted Cottage' competition. *Bus: from Tarnów.*

The museum of folk architecture in Sanok

The dramatic Dunajec Gorge

Dunajec Gorge

The Dunajec Gorge is an 8km
(5-mile) section of the Dunajec
River where its waters squeeze
between steep cliffs, reaching up to
300m (984ft) in height. At its
narrowest, the channel is just 12m
(39ft) wide, creating optimum
conditions for rafting. While not
quite a white-water adrenaline ride,
a raft trip down the gorge is a great
experience and recommended if you
are in this neck of the woods. Rafts
depart the village of Kąty as soon
as they have ten people on board, and
in summer you'll never have to wait
long for one to leave.
*Around 250 rafts ply the river
May–Oct.*

Krynica

Often called Krynica-Zdrój, this quiet
town set amid wooded hills is one of
Poland's best spas and a popular resort
in all seasons. The place to sample the
local mineral-rich water is the Pump
Room. This modern building houses
fountains and the taps from which the
aqua mineralis gurgles. One of these
taps emits Zuber, allegedly the most
concentrated mineral water in Europe,
and definitely an acquired taste. The
other tourist attraction is the **Nikifor
Museum**, which celebrates the life and
work of Nikifor, a self-taught painter
born in the late 19th century. The
exhibition is housed in a timber
building known as the Romanówka.

(*cont on p84*)

Wooden churches of southern Poland

An architectural feature that visitors will notice all across the south of Poland is the wooden churches found in rural areas. Many of these remarkable, almost fairy-tale buildings are so precious that they now come under UNESCO protection. They are one of the unique aspects of travel in Poland, and a few weeks seeking out these timber places of worship on a route across the south of rural Poland makes for an exciting voyage of discovery, and gives a real insight into life away from the Westernised cities.

Wooden churches are a common sight in this region of Poland

History

The majority of these churches were built between the 15th and 19th centuries. They were usually sponsored by the local gentry and represented an affordable and easily built alternative to a full-blown stone structure. What masons in the towns could do with stone, carpenters could easily achieve in wood in half the time. The churches even followed the same development in architectural styles as the stone churches, with Baroque and Renaissance flourishes being added to Gothic forms over the centuries.

Form and materials

Timber structures always seem more in harmony with the surrounding rural scene, especially in mountainous areas. Wooden churches are usually modest affairs, although some impress with their complex architecture. Some of the churches are Eastern Orthodox, and these are easily recognised by their onion domes.

Wooden structures must have dry stone foundations (otherwise they would rot). The best wood to use in

Timber church in Haczów

their construction is larch, thanks to its considerable pitch content, and its ability to resist bad weather, rain, snow and water. Pine, spruce, yew, oak and beech are also used. The vast majority of these churches are constructed using the horizontal log method common in the construction of log cabins. Roofs are made of shingles or occasionally metal. Size was always an issue, and most wooden churches are small affairs. Fire is obviously the timber church's main foe, and some have been lost over the centuries in blazes.

Thanks to their size and the materials used to build them, there is something truly magical about the wooden churches, especially the musty smell and muffled acoustics of their interiors, the neat rows of dark shingles on the roofs, and the time-faded timber of their façades.

Locations

Wooden churches can be found all across southern Poland, from the Tatra Mountains in the west to the border with Ukraine. Małopolska has the greatest concentration, with some of the finest examples situated in Haczów (the largest Gothic timber church in the world), Dębno Podhalańskie, and the areas around Muszyna, Binarowa, Blizne, Lipnica Murowana and Sękowa. Several churches and other examples of timber folk architecture can be found in *skansens* (open-air museums) across Poland.

The Małopolska Tourist Board has come up with a Wooden Architecture Route, 1,500km (930 miles) of trails that go from one wooden building to the next across the province; this includes churches as well as other timber structures. The excellent English-language website dedicated to Małopolska's timber architecture will help you to plan a route of any length (*http://szlak.wrotamalopolski.pl/EN*). Similar churches can be found in eastern Slovakia and west Ukraine.

Nikifor's simple paintings depict scenes from the Beskid area and have a wonderful style all of their own. He always signed his works with a meaningless series of letters.
Nikifor Museum. Bulwary Dietla 19. Tel: 018 471 53 03. Open: Tue–Sun 10am–1pm & 2–5pm. Admission charge. Free on Wed.

Niedzica Castle

Dramatic Niedzica Castle, which occupies a rocky outcrop overlooking the Dunajec Reservoir, started life as a strategic Hungarian border fortress in the 14th century and was given a Renaissance face-lift in the 17th century. Inside, you will discover exhibitions on the castle's history and collections of local folk arts and crafts.
5km (3 miles) west of Kąty. Tel: 018 262 94 89. Open: May–Sept 9am–7pm; Oct–Apr 9am–5pm. Admission charge.

Stary Sącz

Not to be confused with nearby Nowy Sącz to the north, Stary Sącz is one of the oldest settlements in the region and a place closely associated with Princess Kinga, widow of Polish King Bolesław the Shy. She established a convent here in the 13th century and was made a saint in 1999 for her numerous charitable deeds. Kinga is a common girl's name in Poland. The main attractions in Stary Sącz are its cobbled square, the municipal museum and two 13th-century churches. The Gothic parish church was given a thorough Baroque makeover in the 17th century, and the Church of the Poor Clares possesses some 16th-century murals depicting the Blessed Kinga and scenes from her life. Kinga's convent can be found beside the church.
Train or bus: from Nowy Sącz.

Niedzica Castle, one of the most picturesquely situated castles in Poland

The Tatra Mountains above Zakopane

The Tatra Mountains

Around Zakopane (*see p86*), the Tatra Mountains rise to almost 2,500m (8,200ft), creating excellent conditions for strenuous alpine hiking in summer and skiing from early December until March.

Marked trails lead hikers through the mountains, and it is advisable to stick to these at all times while using a map. Wild camping is not permitted in the national park but can be enjoyed elsewhere. Seven huts run by the PTTK also provide high-altitude accommodation. When climbing to the higher reaches, make sure you take all the necessary equipment. Groups of ten or more must be accompanied by a guide. An easy day's walk is to take the cable car from Zakopane to Kasprowy Wierch and walk back down. Longer hikes take you to places such as Morskie Oko, a beautiful alpine lake, or along the Eagle's Path, an exposed ridge. Rysy Mountain in the Tatras is Poland's highest peak at 2,499m (8,199ft).

Ski slopes are graded black, red, blue and green, as at all ski resorts. The most popular slopes are Nosal and Kasprowy Wierch because they are the only ones with ski lifts. Skiing lessons are available at the Nosal Ski School, and skis can be rented at a number of places. Cross-country skiing trails are marked orange.

View over Zakopane

Zakopane

The town of Zakopane, within spitting distance of the highest peaks on the Polish side of the Tatra Mountains, is Poland's premier winter resort and a centre for all kinds of snow fun, above all skiing. The architecture is a mix of 19th-century traditional timber houses and modern touristy buildings. The place heaves with visitors in summer when people come to hike the trails through the Tatra Mountains, and in winter when skiers arrive in their thousands. Despite its status as Poland's favourite alpine retreat, Zakopane failed in its bid to host the 2006 Winter Olympics, but is in the running to host the 2013 World Ski Championships.

The Tatra Museum

Situated on the main street popular with visitors, the Tatra Museum has all kinds of exhibits on the history, ethnography, geology and plant and animal species of the Tatra Mountains. The exhibitions dedicated to local *Górale* folk culture are particularly interesting.
ul. Krupówki 10.
Tel: 018 201 52 205.
Email:
biuro@muzeumtatrzanskie.com.pl.
www.muzeumtatrzanskie.com.pl.
Open: Wed–Sat 9am–5pm,
Sun 9am–3pm.
Admission charge.

Zakopane-style architecture

In the graveyard of the timber Church of St Clement stands the tomb of Stanisław Witkiewicz (1851–1915) – a writer, painter, art theoretician and the architect who developed the distinctive 'Zakopane style' of architecture inspired by traditional wooden structures. Witkiewicz was the father of Witkacy, a famous avant-garde painter, playwright and writer who inhabited the town in the interwar years. Witkiewicz is responsible for many of the timber structures with pointed gables and steep sloping roofs around Zakopane. The Willa Koliba behind the church was his first building and now houses the Museum of Zakopane Style. Here you will find exhibitions of the traditional folk crafts in which Witkiewicz found inspiration, a section on his life, and some examples of furniture he designed.

Museum of Zakopane Style. ul. Kościeliska 18. Tel: 018 201 36 02. Open: Tue–Sat 9am–5pm, Sun 9am–3pm. Admission charge.

Małopolska and the Carpathian Mountains

Typical steep roof in Zakopane

Górale (The Highlanders)

Poland's Highlanders (Górale) are a fascinating ethnic minority found in small areas of the mountainous south. Communities also exist on the Slovak side of the border and, in a wider Carpathian sense, in the Hutsul areas of Ukraine and in some parts of Romania. The Górale have strong folk traditions that they strive to keep alive despite mass emigration to the USA over the last 150 years. The Górale represent one of the most colourful sides of Poland's folk tradition, and their culture is well worth seeking out when in the south of the country.

Although it has been proved that these people originally hail from the Balkans and probably settled here sometime in the 14th to 17th centuries, their language and culture have been shaped by the mountains they inhabit. Their environment has also made them fiercely independent, but almost all would claim to be Poles first, Górale second. Divided into tens of sub-tribes, the Górale inhabit small areas in the mountains, mostly in the Podhale area and the Tatra Mountains. In essence, the Podhale area forms the foothills of the Tatra

The Górale inhabit the harsh environment of the Tatra Mountains

olska and is often the
r overland travellers
s location on the major
ailway line between Berlin
v. Other 'unmissables'
n include Kórnik Castle,
Palace, Rogalin Palace and
al town of Gniezno.
he towns and cities you
axing woodland, rolling
vistas and hundreds of
dotting the landscape.
gouged out by glaciers
f the last ice age.

own as Danzig in German)
st of the three communities
p the Tri-City area (the
eing Sopot and Gdynia).
y the Teutonic Knights
century, Gdańsk had
nember of the Hanseatic
the mid-15th century and
tan city-state enjoying
hanks to trade. After the
Poland in 1772, it was
Prussia until after World
it became the Free City
he port area of Gdańsk
he first shots of World War
d of which the city was
pletely destroyed. The
ntre was painstakingly
the next five decades and
ues to this day. Many will
sk thanks to Lech Wałęsa
darity Movement, which
the city's shipyard.

Royal Way

The Royal Way is the route the kings
of Poland used on their annual visits to
the city to collect taxes. It starts at the
trio of town gates called the Upland
Gate, the Foregate and the Golden
Gate, all dating from different periods.
Passing through the Golden Gate,
you find yourself on Ulica Długa
(Long Street), Gdańsk's grandest
thoroughfare with tall, slender town
houses lining the route and street cafés
spilling onto the pavement. Continuing
down Long Street you will have the
spire of the Main Town Hall in your
sights the whole way (*see opposite*).
At the Main Town Hall, Long Street
suddenly widens out into the Długi
Targ (Long Market), a wide
marketplace lined with even grander

Długi Targ, Gdańsk

A Górale cottage, hidden in the woods

Mountains and is centred on the
town of Nowy Targ. Zakopane is also
a centre of Górale culture as well as
much kitschy imitation.

The Górale enjoy their own
distinctive culture, music, food and
traditional dress. Typical Górale
cuisine is simple and modest, and
reflects the ingredients available
in the mountains. Potatoes and
ewe's cheese feature heavily, as do
sauerkraut, mutton and *oscypek*, a
strong smoked sheep's milk cheese,
rolled into a spindle shape, which can
be bought all over Poland and is a
real delicacy. Many 'highlander'
restaurants have sprung up all over
the country, and while the décor may
not be authentic, the food is.

Górale houses are simple timber
cabins full of chunky carved timber
furniture often arranged around a
large decorated oven. Traditional
dress for women includes a white
blouse with seemingly inflated
sleeves, a wide colourful skirt, a dark
laced-up bodice, a plain or
embroidered pinafore, stockings, and
black leather shoes or boots. For men,
the costume is usually much simpler
and consists of light grey trousers
tucked into leather boots, a white
tunic, a dark waistcoat, and a typical
felt hat of which there are several
types. There are many different
variations and styles that change from
region to region. Other typical clothes
include thick woollen socks, sheepskin
slippers and sheep's wool throws,
shawls and blankets, all of which
make excellent souvenirs.

Thanks to a recent resurgence in
interest in folk and regional culture
across Poland, you can experience
Górale culture almost anywhere in
the country. There are Tatra-style
restaurants even on the Baltic coast,
and poor Górale cart their traditional
goods to markets in Warsaw and
other cities. However, authentic
Górale experiences are found in the
mountains and at events such as the
International Festival of Mountain
Folklore held annually in late August
in Zakopane. Being invited to a typical
Górale wedding is an unforgettable
experience, with traditional music and
dance going on into the early hours.

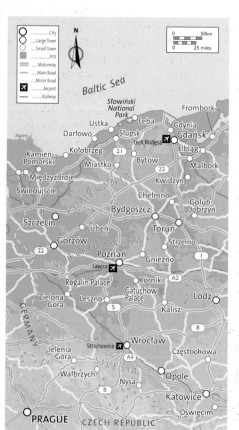

Pomerania and Wielkopolska

The historical territories of Pomerania and Wielkopolska cover a large section of the country to the northwest, bordering the Baltic Sea to the north and Germany to the west. Although physically much the same, with sweeping flat areas of agricultural land, the historical development of the two areas has been quite different.

The highlights for the tourist in this area are the port city of Gdańsk on the Baltic coast, with its rebuilt historical centre, vibrant nightlife and links to Solidarity and the not so distant turbulent history of Poland in the 1980s; Malbork, an enormous red-brick Gothic castle to the south of Gdańsk; and bustling Poznań with its pretty historical centre, large student population and trade fair industry. Diversity is the region's number one draw as a holiday here can combine sightseeing in historical centres, relaxing days on the beach or by a lake, and fun nights out in the region's nightlife hotspots.

POMERANIA

Pomerania is the northern-most of the two provinces, and the northern reaches are lined with the sandy beaches and shifting dunes of the Baltic coast. These run almost unbroken from east of Gdańsk to the border with Germany, and include the Słowiński National Park. Now almost completely Polish, this region was part of Prussia for 200 years until 1919, and this influence is still very much in evidence. In the interwar period, the infamous Polish Corridor to the sea ran through Pomerania, giving Poland access to the port of Gdynia, and Hitler an excuse to invade.

As well as the obvious attractions of the coast, there is a wealth of sights inland. The gigantic castle at Malbork was built by the Teutonic Knights who ruled the area from the 14th to the 16th centuries. Toruń has the best-preserved historical centre, and the rural Kashubian Region, which in places resemb[...] Switzerland a[...] that extends [...] northern Pol[...] minority, the [...] bizarre langu[...] nor German[...] distinct folk [...]

WIELKOPO[...]

'Great Polan[...] cradle of the[...] here that th[...] the 10th cer[...] the Polonia[...] the Piast cla[...] infant state [...] Chrobry th[...] almost all o[...]

With 600[...] is by far the[...]

The Long Market in Gdańsk is lined with grand buildings

in W[...] first [...] than [...] east–[...] and W[...] in the[...] Gatu[...] the ca[...]

Ou[...] will fi[...] agricu[...] scenic[...] These[...] at the [...]

GDA[...]

Gdańs[...] is the [...] that m[...] other t[...] Coloni[...] in the [...] become[...] League[...] a cosm[...] prosper[...] partitio[...] occupie[...] War I w[...] of Danz[...] witnesse[...] II, at the[...] almost c[...] historica[...] rebuilt o[...] work con[...] know Gc[...] and the S[...] was born [...]

A Górale cottage, hidden in the woods

Mountains and is centred on the town of Nowy Targ. Zakopane is also a centre of Górale culture as well as much kitschy imitation.

The Górale enjoy their own distinctive culture, music, food and traditional dress. Typical Górale cuisine is simple and modest, and reflects the ingredients available in the mountains. Potatoes and ewe's cheese feature heavily, as do sauerkraut, mutton and *oscypek*, a strong smoked sheep's milk cheese, rolled into a spindle shape, which can be bought all over Poland and is a real delicacy. Many 'highlander' restaurants have sprung up all over the country, and while the décor may not be authentic, the food is.

Górale houses are simple timber cabins full of chunky carved timber furniture often arranged around a large decorated oven. Traditional dress for women includes a white blouse with seemingly inflated sleeves, a wide colourful skirt, a dark laced-up bodice, a plain or embroidered pinafore, stockings, and black leather shoes or boots. For men, the costume is usually much simpler and consists of light grey trousers tucked into leather boots, a white tunic, a dark waistcoat, and a typical felt hat of which there are several types. There are many different variations and styles that change from region to region. Other typical clothes include thick woollen socks, sheepskin slippers and sheep's wool throws, shawls and blankets, all of which make excellent souvenirs.

Thanks to a recent resurgence in interest in folk and regional culture across Poland, you can experience Górale culture almost anywhere in the country. There are Tatra-style restaurants even on the Baltic coast, and poor Górale cart their traditional goods to markets in Warsaw and other cities. However, authentic Górale experiences are found in the mountains and at events such as the International Festival of Mountain Folklore held annually in late August in Zakopane. Being invited to a typical Górale wedding is an unforgettable experience, with traditional music and dance going on into the early hours.

Pomerania and Wielkopolska

The historical territories of Pomerania and Wielkopolska cover a large section of the country to the northwest, bordering the Baltic Sea to the north and Germany to the west. Although physically much the same, with sweeping flat areas of agricultural land, the historical development of the two areas has been quite different.

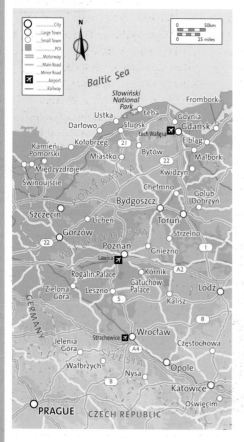

The highlights for the tourist in this area are the port city of Gdańsk on the Baltic coast, with its rebuilt historical centre, vibrant nightlife and links to Solidarity and the not so distant turbulent history of Poland in the 1980s; Malbork, an enormous red-brick Gothic castle to the south of Gdańsk; and bustling Poznań with its pretty historical centre, large student population and trade fair industry. Diversity is the region's number one draw as a holiday here can combine sightseeing in historical centres, relaxing days on the beach or by a lake, and fun nights out in the region's nightlife hotspots.

POMERANIA

Pomerania is the northern-most of the two provinces, and the northern reaches are lined with the sandy beaches and shifting dunes of the Baltic coast. These run almost unbroken from east of Gdańsk to the border with Germany, and include the Słowiński National Park. Now almost completely Polish, this region was part of Prussia for 200 years until 1919, and this influence is still very much in evidence. In the interwar period, the infamous Polish Corridor to the sea ran through Pomerania, giving Poland access to the port of Gdynia, and Hitler an excuse to invade.

As well as the obvious attractions of the coast, there is a wealth of sights inland. The gigantic castle at Malbork was built by the Teutonic Knights who ruled the area from the 14th to the 16th centuries. Toruń has the best-preserved historical centre, and the rural Kashubian Region, which in places resembles low-lying areas of Switzerland and is part of the lake belt that extends across the whole of northern Poland, is home to an ethnic minority, the Kashubians, who speak a bizarre language that is neither Polish nor German. They also have a very distinct folk culture.

WIELKOPOLSKA

'Great Poland' is often called the cradle of the Polish nation as it was here that the Polish nation emerged in the 10th century. A Slav tribe called the Polonians (hence Poland), ruled by the Piast clan, formed the core of the infant state, but under Bolesław Chrobry this was extended to take in almost all of what is now Poland.

With 600,000 inhabitants, Poznań is by far the largest urban settlement

The Long Market in Gdańsk is lined with grand buildings

in Wielkopolska and is often the first stop for overland travellers thanks to its location on the major east–west railway line between Berlin and Warsaw. Other 'unmissables' in the region include Kórnik Castle, Gatuchów Palace, Rogalin Palace and the cathedral town of Gniezno.

Outside the towns and cities you will find relaxing woodland, rolling agricultural vistas and hundreds of scenic lakes dotting the landscape. These were gouged out by glaciers at the end of the last ice age.

GDAŃSK

Gdańsk (known as Danzig in German) is the largest of the three communities that make up the Tri-City area (the other two being Sopot and Gdynia). Colonised by the Teutonic Knights in the 14th century, Gdańsk had become a member of the Hanseatic League by the mid-15th century and a cosmopolitan city-state enjoying prosperity thanks to trade. After the partition of Poland in 1772, it was occupied by Prussia until after World War I when it became the Free City of Danzig. The port area of Gdańsk witnessed the first shots of World War II, at the end of which the city was almost completely destroyed. The historical centre was painstakingly rebuilt over the next five decades and work continues to this day. Many will know Gdańsk thanks to Lech Wałęsa and the Solidarity Movement, which was born at the city's shipyard.

Royal Way

The Royal Way is the route the kings of Poland used on their annual visits to the city to collect taxes. It starts at the trio of town gates called the Upland Gate, the Foregate and the Golden Gate, all dating from different periods. Passing through the Golden Gate, you find yourself on Ulica Długa (Long Street), Gdańsk's grandest thoroughfare with tall, slender town houses lining the route and street cafés spilling onto the pavement. Continuing down Long Street you will have the spire of the Main Town Hall in your sights the whole way (*see opposite*). At the Main Town Hall, Long Street suddenly widens out into the Długi Targ (Long Market), a wide marketplace lined with even grander

Długi Targ, Gdańsk

The Neptune Fountain in front of the Artus Court in Gdańsk

buildings. This is where you will find the Artus Court and the Neptune Fountain (*see p94*). The Royal Way ends at the Green Gate (which isn't green at all), which fills the eastern end of the Long Market. Built to accommodate the monarch during visits to the city, the only Polish head of state to use the Green Gate was Lech Wałęsa when he was president.

Artus Court

By far the grandest façade on the Long Market, the Artus Court with its three bold Gothic arches was built in the late 15th century as a meeting place for merchants and other VIPs. Blasted to dust in 1945, Gdańsk's most desirable address was meticulously restored to its former glory and is now open for the public to view its grand main hall and adjoining chambers, which contain some fine examples of 18th-century furniture. The upper floors hold an exhibition on the history of the building.

Main Town Hall and Museum

The original structure of the Main Town Hall dates from the 14th century but has been added to considerably over the centuries. Only the outer walls survived World War II, and this architectural gem was completely rebuilt in the post-war years. It is now home to the Gdańsk History Museum, containing a collection of period rooms, the most outstanding of which is the Red Room with its magnificent decoration and painted ceiling. The room is an original as it was taken to pieces and hidden during World

The Gdańsk Crane at the waterfront

War II. The second floor houses exhibits on the history of the city.
ul. Długa 47. Tel: 058 767 91 00. Open: Tue–Sat 10am–4pm, Sun 11am–4pm. Admission charge.

Neptune Fountain

The black figure of Neptune wielding his trident and created in the early 17th century by Flemish sculptor Peter Husen survived World War II by being hidden away with many other treasures. It's a common meeting place and the focal point of life in Gdańsk.

The waterfront and Maritime Museum

The Gdańsk waterfront was once busy with barges loading and unloading their cargoes of grain and wood. Now it teems with strolling tourists enjoying the views of the river and the street cafés and restaurants. The main attraction is the Gdańsk Crane, a wooden structure that was the largest crane in medieval Europe. The mechanism inside was powered by people walking around huge wheels like mice. The crane is part of the Maritime Museum, which has various exhibits on both sides of the Motława River including an exhibition of boats from around the world, a section on Poland's seafaring history and the *Sołdek*, the first ship to be built in Gdańsk following World War II.
ul. Ołowianka 9–13. Tel: 058 301 86 11. www.cmm.pl. Open: Tue–Sun 10am–3pm. Admission charge.

The Solidarity Movement

In July 1980, following price rises announced by the communist government, a wave of strikes broke out across Poland. This followed a decade of disquiet as the economy stumbled and the national debt rose. The biggest strikes paralysed the Silesian coal mines and the Gdańsk Lenin Shipyard, and it was at the latter that the communists were forced to accept the right of the workers to form trade unions and to hold strikes. Thus Solidarity (or Solidarność) was born, a movement that would eventually bring the whole of the communist Eastern Bloc crashing down. Its leader was Gdańsk Shipyard electrician Lech Wałęsa.

In its early days, Solidarity had an incredible 10 million members. It had to perform a delicate balancing act between providing a non-party platform for discussion of topics that had been taboo since World War II, while keeping onside with the communist authorities.

All this ended in December 1981 when Polish prime minister General Jaruzelski, perhaps fearful of military action by the USSR, declared a state of martial law, and Solidarity was banned. Its leaders, including Lech Wałęsa, were thrown into jail and arrests continued until 1986, even though martial law was lifted in 1983. Mikhail Gorbachev's rise to power in the USSR led to a relaxing of the Communist Party's grip in Poland. In April 1989, Solidarity, the Church and the government were party to the Round Table Agreements which led to the June elections, the first in the communist world to allow a real political alternative to the communists to stand. In a domino effect, by the end of the year the Berlin Wall was down and regimes from Czechoslovakia to Romania had been swept aside by mass movements calling for democratic reforms and freedom. Lech Wałęsa went on to serve as Polish president from 1990 to 1995, though he and Solidarity have since fallen off the radar as a political force in the country.

The Solidarity logo

Church of St Mary

From the air, the Church of St Mary stands out as the largest structure in the historical centre and may be the largest Gothic red-brick church in the world, able to hold up to 25,000 people. The austere interior holds a huge astronomical clock dating from 1470, and various ornate chapels. The tower can be climbed for bird's-eye views of the old centre.

Gdańsk Shipyard

To the north of the Old Town, you will find the famous Gdańsk Shipyard. Though access to the shipyard itself is prohibited, there are two interesting sights at its gates. The first is the Monument to Fallen Shipyard Workers. The three 42m (138ft) high crosses remember those killed in the strikes of 1980. Behind that is the Roads to Freedom Museum, where black and white photos, news clippings, recordings and artefacts from the period are used to tell the Solidarity story. Highlights include a mock-up of a communist-era grocer's shop, a bust of Lenin, and footage from the period Poland spent under martial law in the early 1980s.

The Church of St Mary dominates the centre of Gdańsk

ul. Wały Piastowskie 24. Tel: 058 308 44 28. Open: May–Sept Tue–Sun 10am–5pm; Oct–Apr Tue–Sun 10am–4pm. Admission charge.

Great Mill

The Great Mill, a bizarre building in the heart of the Old Town, was erected in the mid-14th century by the Teutonic Knights and was the largest mill in Europe for many centuries. Only World War II halted the machinery inside. Rebuilt in the 1960s, its giant slanting roof now covers a shopping mall.

Mariacka Street

This street running from the waterfront to the Church of St Mary is often described as the prettiest in Poland. In 1945 it was reduced to rubble by Red Army shells but has since been rebuilt using old plans and photographs. It is now an atmospheric place lined with cafés, craft shops and amber stalls.

Oliwa Cathedral

Situated 7km (4 miles) west of the city centre in the Oliwa district of Gdańsk, the Oliwa Cathedral dates back to 1178. Originally built by the Cistercian Order, it is a true mix of styles with a Baroque entrance wedged between two red-brick octagonal Renaissance towers, and a lofty Gothic interior. It houses a magnificent rococo organ with 7,896 pipes, which is used at free concerts several times a day in

The Monument to Fallen Shipyard Workers

summer. The cathedral is surrounded by a relaxing park littered with pieces of modern sculpture.
Train: take the SKM commuter train from Gdańsk Main Station, alighting at Oliwa station, then walk 500m (550yds) west.

Westerplatte

The Westerplatte at the mouth of the River Motława is famous for being the place where the first shots of World War II, fired from the ship the *Schleswig-Holstein*, rang out at dawn on 1 September 1939. The garrison of Polish soldiers held out for a week against the might of the Nazi navy. To commemorate this valiant act, a monument in the socialist realism style was erected. Across the river stands the old lighthouse from where the Germans also fired on the garrison. *Bus: 106; Boat: from Gdańsk waterfront.*

FROMBORK

The principal attraction in Frombork is the Cathedral Hill complex, which has a close association with Nicolaus Copernicus. It was here that he spent the latter half of his life and did much of his famous work. Frombork was the seat of the Warmian Bishops from the 13th century, and it was they who fortified the strategic hill. The cathedral survived many invasions and even World War II, which razed the town below to the ground.

Nicolaus Copernicus Museum

The main exhibition dealing with Copernicus' life and work is housed in

Cathedral Hill, Frombork

the Bishop's Palace. Other sights belonging to the museum include the cathedral, the belfry, Copernicus' Tower (housing a mock-up of the astronomer's study), and the Southern Gate containing the ticket office. The cathedral is an impressive Gothic structure lined with Baroque altars and home to an organ used to give summer concerts. Copernicus is buried here, but no one knows the exact location.
ul. Katedralna 8. Tel: 055 244 00 71. www.frombork.art.pl. Open: daily 9am–4pm. Admission charge.

MALBORK CASTLE

One of the must-see attractions in northern Poland is the mammoth red-brick Gothic castle of Malbork, approximately 50km (30 miles) south of Gdańsk. It was built by the Teutonic Knights in the late 13th century, and served as their capital for the next 200 years. After that, it came into the hands of the Polish kings who stayed here for three centuries during their tax-collecting missions from Warsaw to Gdańsk. The Prussians moved in following the Partition of Poland in the late 18th century, and during their time here the castle was renovated in the neo-Gothic style. Used as a prisoner of war (POW) camp for Commonwealth soldiers until 1945, many parts were reduced to rubble by a Red Army bombardment from across the Nogat River. Much has been painstakingly rebuilt, although in many parts of the

The enormous Malbork Castle complex

huge complex of buildings this is still a work in progress.

The castle can only be entered with a guide, and tours are available in Polish, English, German and Russian. The castle is so vast that it can take up to three hours to see everything. After crossing the first drawbridge, the tour starts in earnest in the large courtyard of the Middle Castle. To the right is the Grand Masters' Palace and to the left several renovated spaces house exhibitions, including one on local amber. Moving on from the Middle Castle, another drawbridge under a portcullis leads to the smaller courtyard of the High Castle, the oldest part of the fortress. Here you will find the Chapterhouse, the Treasury and the Church of Our Lady, which will be undergoing restoration for many years to come. The last remaining highlight is the Main Tower, which can be climbed for superb views. After the long tour, you may welcome a break at the Piwniczka Restaurant within the castle walls, or a stroll over the wooden footbridge across the wide river for the best views of the castle in its entirety.

Malbork Castle Museum. Tel: 055 647 09 78. www.zamek.malbork.pl. Open: Apr–Sept Tue–Sun 9am–7pm; Oct–Mar Tue–Sun 10am–3pm. Admission charge.

Drive: Along the Baltic coast

This drive follows the scenic Baltic coast from Gdańsk to the Słowiński National Park via Sopot, the Hel Peninsula and Łeba.

Allow at least half a day.

Begin on the main dual carriageway from Gdańsk through the Tri-City.

1 Sopot

Your first stop is the seaside resort of Sopot, with its bustling café-lined Bohaterów Monte Cassino Street, leading down to Europe's longest wooden pier that juts 500m (1,640ft) out into the Baltic. During the short Baltic summer, Sopot's beach is definitely the place to be and the town has one of the most vibrant nightlife scenes in Central and Eastern Europe.

Continue northwards along the dual carriageway to Gdynia.

2 Gdynia

The port of Gdynia is worth just a short stop to see the seafront and

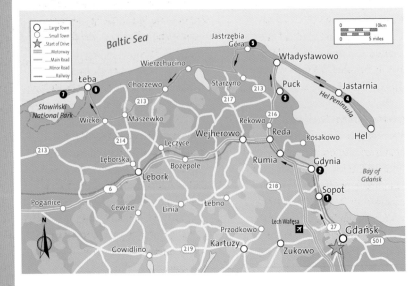

enjoy the busy shopping streets.
Gdynia was a small fishing village
until the interwar years, when it found
itself at the end of the so-called Polish
Corridor, making it the ideal place
to build a port. The town has some
fine examples of modern interwar
architecture, and wide sandy beaches
to the south.

*Rejoin the dual carriageway and head
for Reda, where you should turn off
north onto route 216 for Puck.*

3 Puck

This pretty little Kashubian fishing
port was the headquarters of the
Polish navy from 1567 until the
Partition of Poland. It was Poland's
only port in the early years of the
Polish Corridor.

The main attraction is the red-brick
Gothic Church of SS Peter and Paul
picturesquely overlooking the fishing
harbour. The town also has two
wooden piers and a small beach.

*Continue north on route 216, heading
east at the town of Władysławowo to
access the Hel Peninsula.*

4 Hel Peninsula

This is a thin strip of sand that
arches out almost 30km (19 miles)
into the Bay of Gdańsk. In some
places it is hardly wide enough to
accommodate the road and rail
track that run its length, in others
it is sufficiently substantial to
support a small town. At the tip
of the sandbank lies the tiny fishing

community of Hel itself, where the
main attractions are its location,
the kilometres of beach and a small
seal sanctuary.

*Retrace your route back along the
peninsula, then carry on past
Władysławowo along the coast.*

5 Jastrzębia Góra

The high sandy cliffs at this tiny
resort provide views across the
Baltic. It is also a good place to
have a meal.

*Head back inland until you reach
route 213, then head west to Łeba.*

6 Łeba

The old fishing village of Łeba
(pronounced *weba*) is one of the
Baltic's finest resorts, with kilometres
of dunes, beaches and forests lining
the coast. Things get busy here in
summer, but there's enough sand in
either direction to escape the crowds.
Łeba is the gateway to the Słowiński
National Park.

*Park the car in Łeba and walk the
1.5km (1 mile) to the park entrance at
Rabka, or drive there.*

7 Słowiński National Park

The park west of Łeba is known best
of all for its picturesque beaches and
shifting dunes, some of which reach
almost 40m (130ft). Most of the park
is, however, made up of two lagoons
called Łebsko and Gardno, which
are protected from the Baltic by
the dunes.

THE BALTIC COAST
Darłowo

Around 50km (31 miles) west of the dunes of the Słowiński National Park, the first of many resorts worth a stop-over is Darłowo. The town is set back about 2km (1¼ miles) from the sea where you will find Darłówko (Little Darłowo). Apart from the beaches to the north of the town, Darłowo has a pleasant historical centre worthy of a few hours' exploration.

The town square, lined with Baroque and Renaissance town houses, accommodates two of the town's sites, the Renaissance town hall and the Church of St Mary. The latter is built in the red-brick Gothic style common across northern Poland. To the south of the square stands the 14th-century castle of the Dukes of Pomerania. Inside, you will discover a museum with exhibitions devoted to local folk crafts and traditions, and period furniture. To the northeast of the square stands the 12-sided Chapel of St Gertrude dating from the 17th century.

Kamień Pomorski

Sheltered from the Baltic currents in the Kamieński Lagoon, approximately 100km (62 miles) west of Darłowo, lies the sleepy town of Kamień Pomorski. From its current state of drowsiness you would certainly never guess that this was once the seat of the bishopric of Pomerania and a member of the Hanseatic League.

All the town's historical sights are situated near the waterfront around the main square, which is dominated by the 15th-century town hall. The most famous building is the Cathedral

Darłowo's castle, former home of the Dukes of Pomerania

Ustka beach near Darłowo

of St John the Baptist east of the square. The original structure dates back to the late 12th century and has been added to over the centuries. Inside, a wonderful altar and a Baroque organ catch the eye. Across from the cathedral you will notice the late Gothic Bishop's Palace. The only other place of interest is the Wolin Gate, which once formed part of the town walls and is now home to the Museum of Precious Stones.

Międzyzdroje

This resort lies on the Baltic coast of the Wolin Island, which is formed by the large Szczeciński Lagoon, the small Kamieński Lagoon and the River Dziwna. Much of the island is occupied by the Wolin National Park.

Międzyzdroje (pronounced *Myondzi-zdroyeh*), the best base for discovering the island on foot, is one of the Baltic coast's favourite resorts

and attracts crowds of sun seekers in the summer months. Out of season it's a quiet place, when the charms of the island and the trails that criss-cross it can be enjoyed even more. Międzyzdroje has some superb beaches and surprisingly warm seas in July and August.

Świnoujście

The port and beach resort of Świnoujście (pronounced *Shvinowshche*) lies across the channel that divides Wolin from the much bigger island of Uznam. The town only just makes it into Poland, as the majority of the island is German territory. The beach and spa are the main attractions in a fairly unremarkable town. Ferries can be taken from here to Sweden and Denmark, and there is a border crossing into Germany 3km (2 miles) west of the town.

Amber of the Baltic coast

Amber is picked up on beaches across northern Poland, the Russian enclave of Kaliningrad and the Baltic states. Although it looks like a stone, amber is in fact fossilised resin that oozed out of a tree 40–60 million years ago. As it travelled, the amber enveloped leaves, twigs and insects in a gooey trap, and these can be seen today through the transparent yellow glass-like 'stone'. Whole large insects can be found in some pieces (even whole lizards encased in amber exist), but most contain tree debris, leaves and occasionally flowers and feathers. The far-fetched premise for the *Jurassic Park* films was that DNA could be extracted from dinosaur blood held in a mosquito that had become entombed in amber.

Rough amber is an unremarkable pebble when washed up on a beach, but cutting and polishing can transform it into a beautiful object, perfect for making into all kinds of jewellery. Some like chunky pieces on necklaces and bracelets; others prefer dainty earrings and brooches. Amber was a treasured commodity in medieval Europe, used to make all kinds of beautifully decorated religious and secular objets d'art.

The Baltic boasts the largest deposits of amber in the world, hence the popularity of amber across Poland and the region as a whole. There is an abundance of shops selling 'Baltic Gold', but beware of fake amber, which is simple to produce from plastic and even from sugar. Telling fake from real is difficult without damaging the stones. The best advice is not to buy anything that looks too perfect, and always choose a shop over a street stall.

Baltic amber for sale in Kraków

TORUŃ

Authentic medieval cities are a rarity in Poland, and one of the few examples to come out of World War II virtually unscathed is Toruń, a settlement of 200,000 on the banks of the Vistula River. The renovated centre has received a clean-up in the last 15 years, and today the bright red façades of the Gothic buildings are drawing more visitors than ever. A university city and cultural hotspot, Toruń's greatest boast is as the birthplace of Nicolaus Copernicus (or Mikołaj Kopernik, to give him his Polish name). Born in the city in 1473 to a well-heeled merchant, the man who is said to have 'stopped the Sun and moved the Earth' with his heliocentric description of the solar system studied at the University of Kraków. The merchant's house where he was born is one of Toruń's most popular attractions, and the university also bears his name.

Don't leave town without trying the local speciality – Toruń gingerbread (*piernik toruński*) made with flour, honey, spices and eggs. The availability of exotic ingredients such as ginger and cinnamon in Toruń led medieval bakers to invent this treat, which comes in a variety of shapes and sizes. It is available throughout the city and makes a great souvenir.

History

Like so many other towns in this part of the country, Toruń belonged to the Teutonic Knights from the 13th century. They built up the city, which later became a member of the

Medieval Toruń beside the Vistula River

The Old Town Square in Toruń

Hanseatic League and a major trade centre. As in Gdańsk to the north, it was this prosperous period that gave the city its wealth of Gothic architecture. The Prussian Union drove the Knights out of Poland in the mid-15th century, and the Treaty of Toruń ended their rule in the region. Toruń's prosperity continued until the Swedish invasion of the mid-17th century, a major blow for the city and the entire country. Things got steadily worse from then on, with the Partition of Poland cutting off the now Prussian-controlled town from the rest of Poland to the east. Toruń made an earlier return to Poland than most other settlements in the region, as in 1919 it found itself in the Polish Corridor linking landlocked Polish territory to the sea. Miraculously, the Nazis and Red Army did little damage during World War II, leaving the original historical centre intact. This came under UNESCO protection in 1997. After the war, communist blocks were built in the suburbs.

Orientation

All of Toruń's key sights are grouped around the city's two squares, the focal points of the New Town and Old Town. Despite its name, the New Town is almost as old as its neighbour to the west. The Vistula River flows south of the historical centre and the banks are lined with the Old Town walls, some of the best examples to have survived in all Poland. The railway station is to the south across the Vistula River, the bus station to the north of the historical centre.

Bridge Gate near the Vistula

Walk: Old Toruń

This walk will take you from west to east across the historical centre.

Allow at least 2 hours.

Start your tour of Toruń's splendid attractions at the Church of St Mary.

1 Church of St Mary

This 13th-century Franciscan church has a plain red-brick exterior and a soaring Gothic interior illuminated by tall, slender stained-glass windows. *From the church, cross Panny Marii into Old Town Square.*

2 Old Town Square

The hub of life in the city for centuries, the square is still a hive of activity today. Dominating the centre is a mountain of bricks crafted into the Gothic and Renaissance Old Town Hall, originally dating from the late 14th century. It now houses a museum containing exhibitions of medieval crafts, sculpture and paintings. At the southeastern corner of the square stands a statue of Toruń's favourite son, Nicolaus Copernicus, and a fountain graces the southwestern

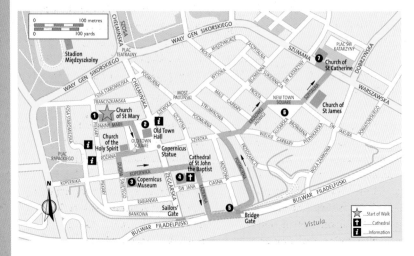

corner near the Church of the Holy Spirit.

Museum. Rynek Staromiejski 1. Tel: 056 622 70 38. www.muzeum.torun.pl. Open: May–Aug 10am–6pm; Sept–Apr Tue–Sun 10am–4pm. Admission charge. Leaving the square by the church, head along Ducha Świętego Street then take a left into Kopernika where you will find the Copernicus Museum on the right.

3 Copernicus Museum

The house where Poland's most celebrated astronomer was born in 1473 today accommodates a museum that looks at his life and work. There's also a fantastic model of the city, which is the centrepiece of a light-and-sound show that transfers onlookers to 14th-century Toruń.

ul. Kopernika 15–17. Open: Tue–Sun 10am–4pm, summer 10am–6pm. Admission charge. Some 200m (220yds) further along Kopernika rises the huge Gothic bulk of the Cathedral of St John the Baptist.

4 Cathedral of St John the Baptist

It took 200 years from 1260 until the mid-15th century to complete this cathedral, and in the tower, one of the last parts to be added, hangs the second-largest bell in Poland, after that of the Church of Our Lady of Licheń. The whitewashed interior is lined with elaborate altars, and the main altar and rose window are

particularly impressive.

From the cathedral, head south towards the river where you will find a long stretch of medieval town walls interrupted by gates.

5 Bridge Gate

The Bridge Gate, as the name suggests, stands where a bridge used to cross the Vistula River from the southern bank to the city centre. The two other gates to the west are called the Sailors' Gate and the Monastery Gate.

From the river, follow the line of the town walls north, then make your way along ul. Królowej Jadwigi to the New Town Square.

6 New Town Square

Certainly less spectacular than its counterpart in the Old Town, the main attraction here is the Church of St James, which has a red-brick exterior complete with rare flying buttresses and a Baroque interior. The church in the middle of the square dates from the 19th century and is now used as a music club.

Some 100m (110yds) east of the New Town Square is the Church of St Catherine.

7 Church of St Catherine

Another place of worship and a major contributor to the Toruń skyline, the garrison Church of St Catherine is a perfectly composed neo-Gothic structure built at the end of the 19th century, and it contains a wonderful altar.

AROUND TORUŃ
Chełmno

Sleepy Chełmno is a real Gothic gem, with original medieval churches and town houses hidden behind an almost complete ring of town walls. This was all built by the Teutonic Knights who had intended to make it their capital.

Most visitors start a tour of the town at the Grudziądz Gate, the only original medieval town gate to have survived. The grid layout of streets leads to the Rynek (main square), where you will find a Renaissance town hall from 1570 housing the regional museum. Of Chełmno's churches, the finest are the huge Gothic parish church just off the

Main street in Gniezno

Rynek, which claims to house genuine miracle-working relics of St Valentine, and the Church of St John the Baptist, part of the Cistercian convent. The town's 2.2km (1⅓ miles) of red-brick town walls encircling the old town are almost the only example in Poland to have survived intact.

Bus: from Toruń or Gdańsk.

Gniezno

You wouldn't know it today, but Gniezno plays an important role in the Polish national identity. This was one of the places where the first Slavic tribes came together to form the cradle of the Polish state in the 10th century. The word *gniazdo* means 'nest' in Polish, and it was here that the mythical Lech found a nest belonging to a white eagle while out hunting, hence the Polish coat of arms. Duke Mieszko I, the grandson of Lech, founded a settlement and was baptised here in AD 966, making Poland a Christian country.

Cathedral

Today, the only site of real interest in Gniezno is the cathedral to the northwest of the main square. Established in AD 997, it was built and rebuilt several times, the last occasion after World War II when it was returned to its Gothic splendour. Inside, there is the sarcophagus of St Adalbert. Adalbert was the second Bishop of Prague who came to Poland as a missionary in 997. Murdered by pagan

Golub Castle

tribes, his body was brought to Gniezno by Bolesław Chrobry and buried in the cathedral two years later. Adalbert was made a saint in the same year, and Gniezno became an archbishopric in 1000. Other highlights include a pair of bronze Romanesque doors and various chapels lining the nave.

Open: May–Sept 9am–5pm; Mar, Apr & Oct 9am–4pm. Closed: Nov–Feb (though access is possible).

Golub-Dobrzyń

As its double-barrelled name suggests, the town is made up of two settlements on the banks of the Drwęca River, united into one town in 1951. Golub dates from the 13th century and has a robust brick Gothic castle with Renaissance trimmings built by the Teutonic Knights. The castle houses a modest ethnographical museum.

Bus: from Toruń.

Kwidzyn

Kwidzyn is another of the region's Gothic-era settlements built up by the Teutonic Knights in the 13th century. The town's two principal sites are the lofty, red-brick cathedral dating from the 14th century with neo-Gothic additions, and the castle, now home to a museum containing exhibitions of medieval religious art and regional folk crafts.

ul. Katedralna 1. Tel: 055 646 3780. www.zamek.malbork.pl/en/kwidzyn/ indexk.php. Open: May–Sept Tue–Sun 9am–5pm, Oct–Apr Tue–Sun 9am–3pm. Admission charge.

Bus or train: from Toruń or Gdańsk.

Strzelno

Strzelno is a small town 25km (15½ miles) to the east of Gniezno. The main attractions here are two Romanesque-era churches, possibly the best in the region.

Bus: from Gniezno.

POZNAŃ

By far the largest city in Wielkopolska and its undisputed capital, Poznań is a vibrant settlement of 600,000 on the banks of the Warta River. Its position on the main Berlin–Warsaw road and rail routes, its flourishing trade fair and conference tourism industry, and a huge student population make this a lively place. The historical centre has one of the finest squares in Poland, and the leafy cathedral precinct on Tumski Island is an oasis of tranquillity.

History

The first settlement appeared here in the 9th century on Tumski Island. By the 13th century, the town had grown rich as it sat at the crossroads of several trans-European trade routes. Decline came with the Swedish invasion of the 17th century, although things did pick up after the First Partition of Poland in the late 18th century when Poznań became the German city of Posen. The local Slavic population resisted Germanisation, and in 1918 Poznań enthusiastically

Houses in Stary Rynek, Poznań

rejoined the Polish state. However, the Germans were back in 1939, and the liberation of the city by the Red Army in 1945 came at a high cost to the population and the historical centre. During food riots in 1956, 76 people were killed by the authorities in Poznań. This was the first significant protest against communist rule in the country.

Orientation

Poznań is a very large city, but thankfully many of the city's places of interest are grouped in the historical core. The chief attraction is the central square of Stary Rynek (Old Marketplace) (*see p115*). The cathedral and the citadel are to the west of the centre.

Cathedral

Around 2km (1¼ miles) northeast of the Stary Rynek (Old Marketplace) stands Poznań's cathedral which has occupied Tumski Island for 1,000 years. Badly damaged in World War II, the whole structure was rebuilt, though allegedly the pre-war building looked very different. Highlights inside include the incredible Renaissance Golden Chapel, built in the 15th century to house the tombs of the first two Polish rulers Duke Mieszko I and Bolesław Chrobry, and the crypt, which is actually the first Romanesque cathedral built on the site. Here, you will find the original resting place of the first Piast rulers, and the tombs of

various bishops of Poznań. The last one was buried here in 1999. Opposite the cathedral stands the Church of St Mary, the oldest in Poznań. Czech Princess Doubrava, who brought Christianity to Poland, had her first chapel here.

Citadel

Poznań's huge citadel is situated 2km (1¼ miles) north of Stary Rynek (Old Marketplace). Built by the Prussians in 1830, it is now a park containing some places of interest and pieces of modern sculpture. It was the scene of fierce fighting between the Nazis and the Red Army in 1945, and part of the citadel is given over to a Red Army cemetery and a final resting place for Commonwealth soldiers killed all over Poland. At the citadel there are two museums, the Museum of Armaments and the Museum of the Poznań Army.
www.city.poznan.pl

Monument to riot victims in 1956

Walk: Old Poznań

This west–east route leads from the Grand Theatre, across Stary Rynek (Old Marketplace) to the Parish Church of St Stanisław.

Allow at least 2 hours.

1 Grand Theatre

Your walk starts at the Grand Theatre, which dates from 1910. The theatre is Wielkopolska's top opera venue.
From here, head through Adam Mickiewicz Park to ul. Św. Marcin.

2 Monument to the Victims of June 1956

You will not need to search long for the monument to those killed in the 1956 food riots. Two monolithic crosses rise from the cobbles,

and a stylised eagle's head sits above the words 'For freedom, justice and bread, June 1956'. One of the crosses bears the years in which major anti-communist protests were held.
Just across the road from the monument stands the Kaiserhaus.

3 Kaiserhaus

The Kaiserhaus is the biggest reminder in Poznań that this was German

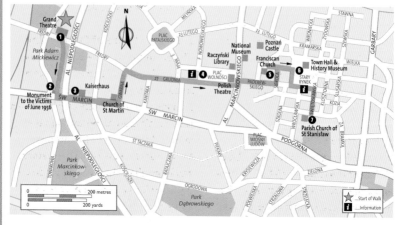

territory for two centuries. It looks ancient, but it was built in the neo-Romanesque style in the early 20th century as a residence for the German Emperor Wilhelm II. The Kaiser didn't get to enjoy it much, and today the building houses an arts centre.
Continue east along ul. Św. Marcin and turn left at the Church of St Martin then right along 27 Grudnia. Within a few moments you will be at the western end of Plac Wolności (Freedom Square).

4 Plac Wolności

To the east of the square stands the Polish Theatre, dating from the 1870s. To the north is the neoclassical Raczyński Library, and to your right stands the **National Museum**, housing the best collection of art outside the capital.
National Museum. al. Marcinkowskiego 9. Tel: 061 856 80 00. www.mnp.art.pl. Open: Tue 10am–6pm, Wed, Fri & Sat 10am–5pm, Thur & Sun 10am–4pm. Admission charge. Free on Sat.
From Plac Wolności, head east along Paderewskiego Street and take a left just before reaching Stary Rynek. Here you will find the Franciscan Church (Church of St Antoni Paderewski).

5 Franciscan Church

The late Baroque Church of St Antoni Paderewski has wonderful decoration and a miracle-working picture of the Virgin Mary. Across from the church are the few remains of Poznań's castle.
Stary Rynek (Old Marketplace) is a few steps downhill from the church.

6 Stary Rynek (Old Marketplace)

The square is dominated by the Renaissance town hall, and every day at noon two mechanical goats lock horns at a window at the top of the façade to commemorate the day the animals saved the building from fire. The building now houses the Poznań History Museum, a good excuse to see the interior. Next to the town hall, the row of pretty façades is called the Fish Sellers' Houses. As you will see, some of the sgraffito decoration is far from ancient. The rest of the square is lined with tall, elaborately decorated town houses, many of which had to be rebuilt at the end of World War II. Street cafés spill out onto the cobbles, and the square is always busy with tourists and shoppers.
Walk out of Stary Rynek, to the south, down ul. Świętosławska.

7 Parish Church of St Stanisław

The beautiful Baroque church at the end of ul. Świętosławska is part of a Jesuit complex that now houses municipal authority offices. The church is Poznań's most elaborate Baroque interior by far, a riot of monster barley-sugar columns, cherubs, stucco and huge altars. In the summer, free organ recitals are given here daily at noon.

AROUND POZNAŃ
Gołuchów Palace

Just a few kilometres outside Kalisz on the Poznań road, this small, fairy-tale, French-style château is worth a short stopoff.

Tel: 062 761 50 94. Open: winter Tue–Sun 10am–4pm. Admission charge. Free Tue & Sat.

Kórnik Castle

The compact neo-Gothic château at Kórnik, surrounded by beautiful parkland and a scenic lake, is one of the highlights of the region and can be found just 20km (12½ miles) southeast of Poznań's city centre. Originally built in the early 15th century, Tytus Działyński, a member of the family that owned Kórnik, gave the building its current appearance in the 19th century. The last owner was Władysław Zamoyski, a Polish patriot who handed over the château and all its precious collections to the Polish people in the 1920s.

The most striking features of the simple but exquisitely furnished interiors are the intricate inlaid parquet floors, the carved portals, a piano that Chopin possibly played, the hefty Gdańsk cupboards, the dining-room ceiling, and the remarkable Moorish columns and archways in the Mauritanian Hall, inspired by the Alhambra in Granada. The chateau is small enough for tours not to be too long, and it is a real must-see for those travelling in the area.

Just off main road to Kalisz.
Tel: 061 817 00 81.
Open: May–Oct Tue–Sun 9am–5pm; Nov–Apr 9am–4pm. Admission charge.

Licheń

Licheń, some 90km (56 miles) east of Poznań, is the second most important pilgrimage site in the country after Częstochowa, attracting almost 1.5 million pilgrims a year. The principal attraction is the Church of Our Lady of Licheń, a mammoth

The Church of Our Lady of Licheń

The beautiful Rogalin Palace

basilica with a great golden dome built to celebrate the millennium, and by far the largest in Poland. In fact, it is Poland's longest, widest and highest church and the 11th longest in the whole world. The superlatives continue in the almost freestanding bell tower, where the biggest bell in the country can be found. The whole project was financed from contributions, and is well worth making the trip to see.

Rogalin Palace

Built in 1768 in the shape of a sweeping neoclassical horseshoe by the Raczyński family, Rogalin Palace is one of the most impressive buildings in Poland. Viewed from the end of an alley of horse chestnut trees that line the approach, it is a truly noble sight. The last owner was Edward Raczyński, who served as Polish president in exile in London during World War II. Part of one of the wings is a mock-up of his flat in London where he lived until the fall of communism. Unfortunately, only two of the wings are open to the public in the main building, with rooms crammed with precious period furniture. The gallery in a separate building contains one of the most outstanding collections of paintings in the country, with works by Matejko, Wyspiański, Bożnańska and Malczewski.

Away from the palace, the Raczyński Mausoleum can be found just off the road, five minutes' walk from the main gate. Behind the palace there are three ancient gnarled oak trees fenced off from the path. These are named Lech, Czech and Rus after the mythical founders of Poland, Bohemia and Rus (now Ukraine). They are at least 1,000 years old.

ul. Arciszewskiego 2, Mosina.
Tel: 061 813 83 57. Open: Tue–Sun
10am–4pm (until 6pm May–Sept).
Admission charge. Free Wed.

Silesia

Śląsko, or Silesia, as it is known in English, occupies the whole of the southwestern corner of Poland, although the wider historical territory extends into North Moravia in the Czech Republic and Saxony in Germany. The area has something for everybody: from sightseeing and culture in Wrocław to witnessing the region's darker side at Oświęcim (Auschwitz), and from hiking the Sudety Mountain range to relaxing at a spa.

History

To understand Silesia fully, one needs to be armed with at least an outline of the region's complicated history. Slavic tribes settled here around AD 500, and Silesia had become part of Poland by the 11th century. The Silesian Piasts encouraged German colonisation of their lands in the early 14th century, setting the scene for future conflicts. Silesian princes aligned themselves with the powerful king of Bohemia, and the Czechs ruled Silesia until 1526 when both Bohemia and Silesia became part of the Habsburg domain. This later became the Austrian Empire despite Swedish and Saxon occupation during the Thirty Years War, which had a devastating effect on the region. The 18th century witnessed the Silesian Wars (1740–42 and 1744–5), which were part of the wider War of Austrian Succession, at the end of which Empress Maria Theresa ceded all of Silesia, except some areas around Opava and Těšín in the Czech lands, to Prussia. Following a plebiscite in 1919 to determine whether Silesia would pass to Poland or be incorporated into Germany, the territory was divided into German Lower Silesia, including Wrocław, and Polish Upper Silesia, including the industrial areas around Katowice. After World War II, the German population was forced to leave, and the whole of Silesia became a province of Poland. West Germany only relinquished official claims to the area under the terms of a pact signed with Poland in 1972.

Highlights and lowlights

Poland's southwestern reaches have some of the country's most attractive architecture and landscapes, as well as some of its worst. On one side of the Silesian coin are its Baroque churches, historical centres, ancient wooded mountains and health-restoring spas. The flipside is the industrial area to the east of the province known as Upper Silesia, particularly the conurbation centred on Katowice, an area devoid of historical sights and avoided by all but the most determined of tourists. This is also where you will find one of Poland's most infamous sites – the death camp at Oświęcim (Auschwitz) – one of the country's most popular tourist destinations.

Historical Wrocław, rich in architecture and culture, is the undisputed capital of Lower Silesia, and a place where most visitors to Silesia find themselves sooner or later. Other attractions are Książ Castle, the Karkonosze National Park and the timber peace churches at Świdnica and Jawor. The area has good transport links to Kraków in the east, Dresden to the west and Prague to the southwest.

WROCŁAW

Wrocław (or Breslau in German) is the capital of Lower Silesia and Poland's fourth-largest city with around 670,000 inhabitants. Built on 12 islands on the Odra River, the city has 112 bridges. It was on Tumski Island that Wrocław was founded in the late 10th century

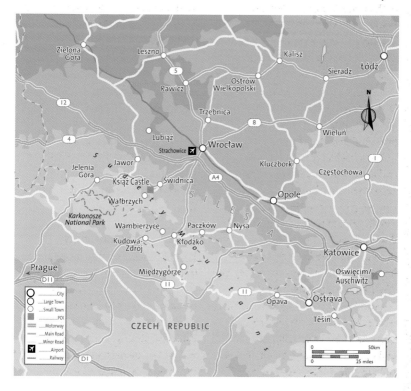

by Duke Mieszko I. In 1000 it became a bishopric. Over the next 900 years the city changed hands many times, with the Tatars, Czechs, Austrian Habsburgs, Prussians and Hitler all holding sway. The Red Army reduced the city to rubble during World War II, and 30 per cent of the population were killed. After the war, the German population was expelled and replaced with Poles from L'viv (Lvov) in what is now Ukraine. Rebuilding work has taken place at the main historical sights, but even in the historical core there is an odd blend of communist-era concrete, rebuilt historical sights and 1990s glass and steel eyesores.

Clock on the front of the town hall on Rynek (*see p122*)

Most visitors only leave the confines of the historical centre to walk over the river to the cathedral. You may need public transport to get from the railway and bus stations to the south of the main square. For the main attractions of the historical centre, see the walking tour (*pp122–3*).

Hala Ludowa (Centennial Hall)

Situated around 3km (2 miles) east of the city centre, this spectacular piece of architecture is worth a look, even if you are not attending a performance. It was built in 1913 by German architect Max Berg to commemorate the 100th anniversary of Napoleon's defeat. The reinforced concrete structure was way ahead of its time, and the huge dome, under which 6,000 people can sit to watch performances, was a truly remarkable feat of engineering. The hall now hosts opera, theatre and music concerts and became Poland's latest UNESCO-listed site in 2006.
ul. Wystawowa 1. Tel: 071 347 51 13. www.halaludowa.wroc.pl. Bus: 145, 146; Tram: 1, 2, 4, 9, 10, 12, 16, 17.

Racławice Panorama

Since it was installed in the 1980s, over 6 million people have visited the Racławice Panorama, making it Wrocław's most popular attraction. The gargantuan canvas (15m/49ft by 114m/374ft), wrapped around the walls of a circular concrete building, tells the story of the Battle of Racławice in

Grand townhouses on the Rynek

1794 between Tadeusz Kościuszko's peasant army and Russian imperial forces. The Poles won the battle but lost the war, and Poland was partitioned. The huge painting shows dramatic battle scenes, and the effect is heightened by cleverly and almost seamlessly combining the canvas with real objects in the foreground.

The history of the canvas is almost as interesting as the events it depicts. Painted in L'viv (Lvov) in the late 19th century by Jan Styka and Wojciech Kossak, it was displayed there until 1944 when it was damaged by a bomb. It came to Wrocław with the L'viv (Lvov) immigrants but, due to its subject matter (Poles defeating Russians), was not exhibited until the Solidarity years of the early 1980s.

ul. Purkyniego 11. Tel: 071 344 23 44. www.panoramaraclawicka.pl. Open: mid-Apr–Aug daily 9am–5pm; Sept & Oct Tue–Sun 9am–5pm; Nov–mid-Apr Tue–Sun 9am–4pm. Admission charge. Audio tours with headphones take place every 30 minutes.

Walk: Old Wrocław

This walk will take you from Plac Solny (Salt Square) to the cathedral on Tumski Island.

Allow at least 2 hours.

Begin your tour at Salt Square.

1 Plac Solny (Salt Square)

The last salt stalls closed almost 200 years ago, but now there is a 24-hour flower market (a Polish speciality). *To the northeast the main square begins, the Rynek.*

2 Rynek (Main Square)

It's difficult to imagine that when the guns went silent in 1945 the entire market square and surrounding streets were left in a heap of smouldering debris. All the grand town houses you see lining the Rynek were rebuilt to look exactly as they did before, sometimes better. The centrepiece is the town hall, which was only partially damaged in the war. The original Gothic building dates from the 13th century, but numerous additions were made until the 20th century when the city council moved out. It's a huge structure and even contains a covered market as well as a museum. In front

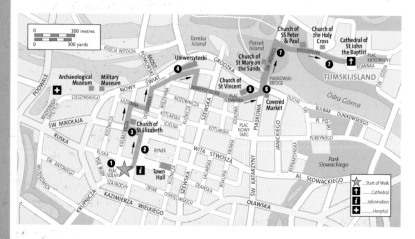

of the main façade you will find the Whipping Post, a copy of an original, where people were flogged in medieval times.

Town hall. Open: Wed–Sun 11am–5pm.

Heading northwest from Rynek, you will arrive at the Church of St Elizabeth.

3 Church of St Elizabeth

The red-brick Gothic Church of St Elizabeth is one of the oldest in Wrocław. The spire is the church's most prominent feature; originally measuring 126m (413ft), the top 36m (118ft) were blown down in a storm. The remaining 90m (295ft) can be climbed for the best views of the historical core. The airy, light interior is also worth a quick look.

Tower. Open: Mon–Sat 9am–4pm, Sun 1–4pm.

From the church, walk north along Odrzańska to the university building on plac Uniwersytecki.

4 Uniwersytecki (University)

The highlight here is the Aula Leopoldinum, an ornate ceremonial hall and Wrocław's finest Baroque interior.

Open: Wed–Mon 10am–3.30pm.

Follow Uniwersytecka Street east to the Church of St Vincent.

5 Church of St Vincent

The grand Gothic Church of St Vincent is the second-largest place of worship in Wrocław. Built on the site of a 13th-century Romanesque basilica, the building was completely destroyed in World War II and only rebuilt in 1991.

6 Covered Market

Opposite the Church of St Vincent sits the covered market, one of the city's most colourful but rarely visited sights. Hundreds of stalls laden with fragrant fruit, vegetables, meat and flowers are spread out under the cavernous arching roof of what resembles a 19th-century railway station but was built in 1908.

Cross the Piaskowski Bridge onto Piasek Island.

7 Piasek and Tumski islands

On Piasek Island you will see the Church of St Mary on the Sands. The vaulting inside is worth a peek. Continue across another bridge to Tumski Island, the site of the original settlement of Wrocław, packed with palaces, churches and administrative buildings. Passing the Church of SS Peter and Paul and the Church of the Holy Cross, which is actually two churches on top of one another, you soon arrive at Wrocław's cathedral dedicated to St John the Baptist, the patron saint of the city. Destroyed in the war, the rebuilt Gothic structure contains many ornate Baroque chapels, and one of the spires can be climbed for views of the cityscape across the Odra.

OŚWIĘCIM (AUSCHWITZ)

Most will not have heard of Oświęcim, an unremarkable industrial town 60km (37 miles) west of Kraków. Arriving at the railway station, there is little to suggest that this was the scene of possibly the greatest atrocity humans ever committed on fellow humans. However, Oświęcim's German name is Auschwitz.

The concentration camp at Auschwitz was built in 1940 on the southern outskirts of the town. At first it was a small-scale affair where Polish political prisoners were kept, but they were soon joined by 12,000 Soviet prisoners of war. It was here that the Nazis began experimenting with Zyklon B gas, and the camp grew as more and more prisoners, now Jews, arrived. The Auschwitz II site, 2km (1¼ miles) to the northwest at Brzezinka (Birkenau), was added in 1941.

The major turning point for Auschwitz was the Wannsee conference of 1942 where the Nazis decided on their 'final solution' – namely the mass extermination of the Jews. The two Auschwitz camps were earmarked as the main centre for their plans. It's estimated that 1.5 million people were murdered here, the vast majority of them Jews. As the Soviets

The entrance to Auschwitz

advanced across Eastern Europe, liberating territory from the Germans, the Nazis tried to erase all evidence of the crimes they had committed at Auschwitz by dynamiting the site. The remains are now a museum.

The camp at Auschwitz I was only partially demolished by the retreating Nazis, and it is here that most people start their tour. The entrance to the main site is through a gate above which is the Nazis' deriding welcome *Arbeit Macht Frei* (Work makes you free). Begin your tour in the cinema where a film shot by the Red Army is shown every 30 minutes. Be warned, however, that the scenes it depicts are of the most harrowing nature, and the museum authorities recommend that children under 14 do not visit the camp. The rest of the buildings are cell blocks and storehouses containing heaps of personal possessions, such as shoes and spectacles, belonging to those who died here. Block 11 is where Zyklon B was first tested on prisoners, and the nearby Death Wall is where thousands of inmates were shot.

The Birkenau camp saw the majority of the genocide committed in Auschwitz, and here you will find the railway tracks leading so ominously to the camp gates where the horrific selection process would take place shortly after transports arrived. Only 60 of the original 300 buildings remain, and these can be seen from the tower at the gate. The Nazis failed to completely destroy the gas

Railway tracks leading to Birkenau

chambers at the far end of the camp, and many of the barracks remain as they were 60 years ago. The cloudy grey pond to the north of the camp is where the ashes of the murdered prisoners were dumped.

Few will leave Auschwitz unaffected by what they have seen. It is the sheer scale of the murdering process that the Nazis established here that is hardest to comprehend.

Tel: 033 843 2133.
www.auschwitz-muzeum.oswiecim.pl.
Camp open daily Dec–Feb 8am–3pm; Mar & Nov 8am–4pm; Apr & Oct until 5pm; May & Sept until 6pm; June–Aug until 7pm.

AROUND WROCŁAW
Jelenia Góra

The town of Jelenia Góra (Deer Mountain) is located some 110km (68 miles) west of Wrocław and is the gateway to the Karkonosze Mountain range. The town's main attractions are its central square (plac Ratuszowy), lined with Renaissance, Baroque and neoclassical town houses, the 15th-century parish church, the Church of the Holy Cross with its beautiful frescoes, and the **Karkonosze Museum** with its glass exhibition.

Museum: ul. Jana Matejki 28.
Tel: 075 752 34 65.
www.muzeumkarkonoskie/pbox.pl.
Open: Tue–Fri 9am–4pm, Sat & Sun 9am–5pm. Closed: Mon. Admission charge. Train or bus: from Wrocław.

Książ Castle

Touristy Książ Castle, 75km (47 miles) southwest of Wrocław and almost in Wałbrzych, is much promoted by the tourist authorities but can prove slightly disappointing. Perched on a rocky promontory high above the Pełcznica River, it creates a dramatic picture with its enormous pink façades behind which hide 400 rooms. Hide is an apt word, as only a fraction of the castle is accessible to the public.

The castle is a hotchpotch of styles from the 13th-century original fortress to 20th-century additions, and every style in between. Apart from the view from the outside, the most impressive part of the castle is the ornate

Inside Książ Castle

Baroque Maximilian Hall. The tower can only be visited as part of a tour in Polish. A medieval stronghold and noble residence, Książ also served as a Wehrmacht headquarters, and the Red Army stayed here a suspiciously long time after World War II. Local rumour has it that they were searching for something, but exactly what remains a mystery.

Tel: 074 664 38 34. Open: Apr–Sept Mon–Fri 10am–5pm, Sat & Sun 10am–6pm; Oct–Mar Tue–Fri 10am–3pm, Sat & Sun 10am–4pm. Admission charge.

Lubiąż

Incongruously located in the middle of the Silesian countryside, the Cistercian abbey complex near the sleepy village of Lubiąż is one of the largest in Europe, with 365 rooms and a façade measuring 223m (732ft) across. When it comes to religious buildings in Poland, size does seem to matter. Originating in the 12th century, the megalomaniac Baroque structure we see today dates from a period of prosperity that the Cistercians enjoyed here following the Thirty Years War. It may become one of the country's finest tourist stops, but after having been used as a stud farm, hospital, arsenal, and many other functions following the decline of the monastery under Protestant Prussian rule, much of the building is in a state of semi-dereliction. Several rooms are open to the public and there is a small museum.
Tel: 071 322 21 29.
www.fundacjalubiaz.org.pl. Open: Apr–Sept daily 9am–6pm; Oct–Mar 10am–3pm. Admission charge.
50km (31 miles) west of Wrocław.

Trzebnica

Another Cistercian abbey can be found in the small town of Trzebnica, 25km (15½ miles) north of Wrocław. The abbey is a popular place of pilgrimage as it was here that St Jadwiga, the patron saint of Silesia, lived out her last years in the convent she founded in 1202. The Basilica of St Jadwiga is thought to be one of the first brick structures built in Poland. Originally constructed in the Romanesque style, it now has Baroque wedding-cake additions. Inside the abbey, there is a wonderful Baroque altar, to the side of which you will find the ornate St Jadwiga's Chapel containing the saint's tomb.

Książ Castle, a popular tourist spot

THE SUDETY MOUNTAINS
Karkonosze Mountains

The Sudety Mountains form the border between Poland and the Czech Republic. The best-known range within the Sudety is the Karkonosze Mountains south of Jelenia Góra. The small area of peaks, some of which rise more than 1,600m (5,250ft), is prime hiking and cross-country skiing territory, and it is for these two activities that most people come. The two principal settlements are Karpacz and Szklarska Poręba, to the south of which lies the Karkonosze National Park on the border with the Czech Republic. These are the higher reaches of the range that include the highest mountain in Silesia, Śnieżka (1,602m/5,256ft), which is cut in half by the border line. This is one of the most popular hiking destinations, but at 270m (886ft) higher than Ben Nevis in Scotland, this is a mountain and an area to be taken seriously, especially in winter. The climate can be unkind in these parts, with heavy rain, and snow on the peaks for six months of the year. Find a good map, don some stout boots and pack all the necessaries into your rucksack before heading off along the well-marked trails that criss-cross the area.

Kłodzko

Kłodzko is the largest town in the middle of a part of Poland that protrudes around 50km (31 miles) into the Czech Republic known as the Ziemia Kłodzka, an area of wooded hills dotted with small spa towns. This is one of Silesia's oldest settlements, and its historical core is worth a few hours' perusal. There is an attractive main square, a Gothic bridge adorned with Baroque statues resembling Charles Bridge in Prague, and a few pieces of Baroque architecture, including the remarkable interior of the Church of the Virgin Mary. However, the town's main attraction is the fortress, considerably beefed up by the Prussians in the 18th century. A system of tunnels dug by prisoners of war during Prussian rule, and the views across the town from here, should not be missed.

Kłodzko Fortress. Tel: 074 867 34 68. Open: 9am–6pm. Admission charge.

Karkonosze Mountains

Kudowa Zdrój

The Polish word *zdrój* means 'spa', and Kudowa Zdrój is the most popular health resort in the Ziemia Kłodzka. Pressed tight against the border with the Czech Republic, the town has a couple of attractions as well as its mineral water and spa treatments. The spa park in the centre of town is a relaxing expanse of greenery, and here you will find the pump room dispensing the local spring water.

The Museum Zabawek 'Bajka' (toy museum) will keep adults and children alike entertained for an hour or so, and then you can walk north to see the Chapel of Skulls (perhaps without the children). The interior is lined with skulls and bones of people who died over the centuries from the plague or in the many wars to have swept through the region. It is a creepy sight and not for the squeamish! The chapel is similar to the ossuary in Kutná Hora over the border in Bohemia.

Muzeum Zabawek 'Bajka'.
ul. Zdrojowa 46B. Tel: 060 177 33 62.
Open: Jan–Mar 10am–4pm; Apr–Dec 9am–5pm. Admission charge.

Silesia

Kłodzko Fortress

Międzygórze

This village, whose name aptly means 'Between the Mountains', is located at the head of a valley in the Ziemia Kłodzka, and provides an excellent base for exploring the Śnieżnik, the highest point in the area. The most striking feature of the settlement is its timber architecture. Built in the early 19th century, these guesthouses are still in use by tourists and walkers. There is a picturesque 21m (69ft) high waterfall just west of the centre.
Bus: from Kłodzko.

Nysa

This town of 50,000 on the banks of the Nysa Kłodzka River was once one of the most important religious centres in central Europe. During the Counter-Reformation in the 17th century, the

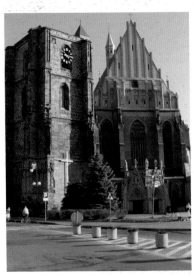

Cathedral of SS James and Agnes, Nysa

bishops of Wrocław, forced out by the Protestants, made Nysa their power base. This generated a building boom that led to Nysa sometimes being dubbed the 'Rome of Silesia'. Unfortunately some 80 per cent of the town was flattened during World War II, and although many buildings were resurrected, the town lost much of its atmosphere and appeal.

Most of the sights are grouped around the central marketplace. The most striking building is without doubt the imposing Cathedral of SS James and Agnes, which was built in just six years in the early 15th century. Completely destroyed in 1945, the interior is now rather austere. The nearby Bishop's Palace houses a museum that exhibits paintings, archaeological finds, photos of the war damage, and a saddening scale model of Nysa in its 17th-century heyday.
Bus: from Kłodzko, Wrocław and Opole.

Paczków

Halfway between Kłodzko and Nysa, the small town of Paczków boasts some of the best-preserved and most complete town walls in Poland and possibly the whole of central Europe. Built in the mid-14th century, they were 9m (30ft) high and encircled by a moat. An extra ring of walls was added with the advent of gunpowder, but this was demolished in the 19th century. Three of the four gates and 19 of the 24 watchtowers have survived. The

The basilica at Wambierzyce

town gives an idea of what most town walls in this part of the world would have once looked like. Only fragments remain in many towns because they were demolished in the 19th century due to the commonly held view at the time that they were strangling economic development. Paczków has somehow managed to hang on to an almost complete set.

Bus: from Nysa and Kłodzko.

Wambierzyce

In a remote location off the road heading northwest from Kłodzko to the Czech border lies the small village of Wambierzyce, another of Poland's Marian pilgrimage sites. The Baroque basilica was built in the 17th century, but Wambierzyce's story starts back in 1218 when a blind man regained his sight after praying before a statue of the Virgin Mary on a lime tree. The site attracts thousands of pilgrims, especially around feast days. There are almost 100 other shrines around the village that lead pilgrims to Calvary, a tree-covered hill opposite the basilica.

Bus: from Kłodzko.

Inside Jawor peace church

UNESCO PEACE CHURCHES OF JAWOR AND ŚWIDNICA

Located around 50km (31 miles) apart, the architectural features that bring the Silesian towns of Jawor and Świdnica together are two peace churches, both of which were added to UNESCO's list of World Cultural Heritage Sites in 2001. They are the largest timber-framed religious buildings in Europe, built by Protestants on Catholic Habsburg territory according to conditions laid out in the Peace of Westphalia, which ended the Thirty Years War. In their typical bureaucratic style, the Habsburgs stipulated that the churches had to be built out of town using only timber, clay and straw and no nails. They were not permitted to have a belfry or bells, the dimensions of the

buildings were strictly prescribed, and all the work had to be carried out within one year. When Silesia came under Prussia in the 19th century, these rules were broken, hence the belfries and brick and stone additions. Three were built in total, but the church in Głogów burned down in 1758. Both make good day trips from Wrocław, but Świdnica is the nearest and easiest to reach and can be combined with a visit to nearby Książ Castle.

Jawor

The small town of Jawor can be found around 80km (50 miles) west of Wrocław. The peace church here is less atmospheric than that of Świdnica, but an impressive sight nonetheless. It was built in 1654 by Albrecht von

Säbisch, who designed the interior with four tiers of galleries on all sides to pack as many people inside as possible. Untypical for a Protestant church are the Baroque decorations with almost every surface painted or carved. The church is still used for services and occasional concerts.
Peace church. Open: Apr–Oct Mon–Sat 10am–5pm, Sun noon–5pm.

Świdnica

Although slightly smaller than Jawor's church, the peace church in Świdnica is the better-known and more frequently visited of the two, possibly because the town is worth a few hours' inspection in its own right. Located to the north of the town centre, the austere but attractive black-and-white timber-frame building conceals a musty Baroque interior with elaborate decoration, tightly packed pews, and galleries on all sides to accommodate the large Protestant congregation (it is claimed 3,500 worshippers could fit inside).

Świdnica has several other places of interest, including the medieval town square with its Baroque façades and town hall, two fountains, and the Gothic Church of SS Stanisław and Wenceslas. After the Thirty Years War, the church came under the control of the Jesuit Order who fitted it out with an elaborate Baroque interior. The belfry at the church is the second highest in Poland at 103m (338ft).
Peace church. www.kosciolpokoju.pl. Open: Apr–Oct Mon–Sat 9am–1pm & 3–5pm, Sun 3–5pm; Nov–Mar call ahead on 074 852 28 14. Admission charge.

The peace church in Świdnica

Getting away from it all

Poland is an ideal destination when it comes to escaping the noise and bustle of the city. Most of the country is rural agricultural land dotted with forests and lakes. The mountainous regions of the south are virtually uninhabited, and the national parks are oases of peace and tranquillity. In the shifting sand dunes of the northern Baltic coast you can walk for kilometres without meeting a single person, and the dark green forests of the east soothe the soul.

MOUNTAINS

The mountain ranges of Poland's underbelly, along the borders with the Czech Republic, Slovakia and Ukraine, offer the best walking, hiking, climbing and mountain-biking possibilities in the country. The highest range is the Tatras (*see pp85–7*), the most remote must be the Bieszczady in the east, and the lowest and most accessible is the Karkonosze in the west. Poland has an excellent system of marked hiking trails, so you shouldn't get lost. Campsites and refuges dot the mountains, and wild camping is permitted except in protected areas. The Tatras are serious alpine terrain, and you should take appropriate clothing and equipment with you, especially in winter and early spring.

The Tatra Mountains

NATIONAL PARKS

Poland has no fewer than 23 national parks spread around the entire country. The following are the best known.

Białowieża National Park

The most famous of Poland's protected areas can be found in the east. This, the last major area of primeval forest left in Europe, covers over 1,200sq km (463 square miles) and extends over the border into Belarus. The European bison held in a special reserve are the biggest draw, and the rest of the forest is stunningly beautiful.

Bieszczady National Park

One of the least visited parks, this remote protected area of hills and mountains in the far southeastern corner of the country is one of the last places in Europe you will see bears, wolves and lynx in the wild.

Karkonosze National Park

A section of the small mountain range known as the Karkonosze has been designated a national park, but the entire mountainous region of the southwest is a great place for light hiking and mountain biking.

Słowiński National Park

Up in the far north to the west of Gdańsk, the most striking features of this area are its dunes and beaches. Black and white storks, the white-tailed eagle, and 250 other species of bird are the park's main attractions for nature-lovers. There are also 600 lakes and the park has been declared a UNESCO Biosphere Reserve. Kluki and Smołdzino are the most interesting villages to head for.

Tatra National Park

The Tatra Mountains, part of the Carpathians, can be found in the far south of the country along the border with Slovakia. Although some of the highest peaks and best scenery are over the border, the Polish side is a superb place to hike in dramatic surroundings. Paths are well marked and no camping is allowed. The gateway to the park is the resort of Zakopane (*see pp86–7*).

WATER

In Europe, only Finland has more lakes than Poland, and numerous rivers flow south to north to the Baltic. You are never far away from a body of water, especially in the north where beautiful sandy beaches line the Baltic. The best rafting and canoeing in Poland is provided by the Dunajec Gorge in the Pieniny mountain range in the south (*see p81*).

Kamienczyk Waterfall, Karkonosze National Park

When to go

It is no exaggeration to say that Poland has something for everyone at any time of year. Many consider spring and autumn the best seasons to visit, but summer on the Baltic coast makes a great holiday, as does winter fun in the snow in the mountainous regions of the south. Whatever season you choose, make sure you bring appropriate clothing – in winter the temperatures can sink well below zero.

Spring

Spring is arguably the most pleasant season of the year to be in this part of the world. The countryside wakes from its long winter slumber, many tourist attractions reopen, and the harsh winter weather becomes a distant memory. The last of the snows melt on

Be prepared for unsettled weather in spring

the central plains (although it lingers a while in the mountains), trees come into blossom, and the traditional *Topienie Marzanny* (drowning of the winter witch) takes place across the country to bid farewell to winter. Easter is celebrated with much more traditional enthusiasm in Slavic countries, and many towns and villages hold fairs and other events at this time. Staunchly Catholic Poland sees the churches full to bursting point for special Easter Masses. The weather can be unpredictable, but it can be rather warm even in May on the plains and in the south. Expect temperatures between 7°C (45°F) and 20°C (68°F), but take off a few degrees in the mountains and by the Baltic. Late spring is also the best time for outdoor activities such as hiking, cycling and horse-riding.

Summer

The tourist season in Poland lasts from May until September, and this is when most visitors will find themselves in the country. The best place to be at this time of year is by the Baltic on the long sandy beaches of the north coast. Unfortunately, this is where most of the Polish population head for on their annual holidays, and things get pretty crowded. Accommodation must be booked well in advance on the coast, especially in July and August. The area around Gdańsk is possibly the best place to go as the city and its conurbation partners,

Blue skies over fields of rape

Sopot and Gdynia, host numerous cultural events at this time of year, and the nightlife is in full swing. Kraków sees its biggest influx of visitors from abroad in the summer months, as does Warsaw. This is also a good time for hiking and climbing in the mountains, and for watersports across Poland.

Expect temperatures ranging from around the low 20s (°C, 70°F) on the coast to the mid to high 20s in the south. The mountains tend to be around 10°C (18°F) cooler in

Autumn can be a good time for sightseeing

summer than locations lower down on the plains.

Autumn

In a similar way to spring, the 'golden Polish autumn', as the Poles call it, can be one of the most pleasant times to be in the country. The weather is not as hot as in July and August, the days are still long, and it rains less. Museums, galleries and other tourist sights are still open, but the crowds are less imposing. In October and November, the forests turn into a fiery mix of vibrant colours. This is by far the best time to be out in rural Poland, hiking in the mountains, watching the farmers bring in the last of the crops, or in the towns and cities observing life revert to its normal course after the summer break. When the nights close in, cosy restaurants and pubs beckon.

Temperatures in autumn range from the low teens (°C, 55°F) in September, to as low as 5°C (41°F) in November (and even lower in the mountains where the first snow can fall as early as late September). Evenings can be chilly everywhere.

Winter

Polish winters can be harsh, with temperatures often remaining below zero for weeks on end, especially on the plains and in the south. The winter weather should never be underestimated and, if travelling at this time of year, you should bring plenty of warm clothing and suitable footwear. Many snow-bound central areas can be cheerless and uninviting in the winter months, but this is certainly not true of the mountainous regions of the south where the skiing season kicks off in early December and ends in March. Skiers and snowboarders could do a lot worse than head for the town of Zakopane in the Tatra Mountains (*see pp85–7*) for some of the best snow fun in central Europe. Kraków (*see pp60–67, 70*) can also be atmospheric under a blanket of snow, as can the historical centres of other towns and cities at Christmas time. New Year is celebrated with gusto across Poland, with much vodka-fuelled merrymaking.

WEATHER CONVERSION CHART

25.4mm = 1 inch

°F = 1.8 × °C + 32

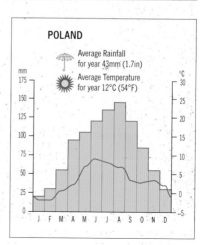

POLAND

Average Rainfall for year 43mm (1.7in)

Average Temperature for year 12°C (54°F)

Getting around

Despite being one of Europe's largest states, Poland is relatively easy to get around using public transport. The trains are clean, efficient and run on time, you can get to even the smallest villages in the mountains by bus, and LOT operates a network of domestic flights. Only Poland's road network could be described as unsatisfactory, and driving here is not for the faint-hearted. Main roads and motorways are being built, but this is proving to be a very slow process.

Centrum metro station, beside the Palace of Culture and Science

By air

Scheduled domestic flights within Poland are operated by the national carrier LOT. Warsaw is linked by air with Bydgoszcz, Katowice, Kraków, Gdańsk, Poznań, Łódź, Szczecin, Wrocław and several other smaller towns. All internal flights go through Warsaw, and there are no direct connections between other cities. Tickets can be booked at LOT and Orbis offices.

By train

There are 27,000km (16,778 miles) of railway track in Poland, and all of it is operated by PKP. Trains are best for long-distance travel between big cities, and services are frequent and fast on main lines. There are various types of train plying Polish tracks. The fastest is the *ekspres*, which runs between major centres. Seats must be booked in advance on these services, as they must on the next category of train, the InterCity (or

EuroCity). These are of a slightly better standard than *ekspres* trains, and run between major cities within Poland (InterCity) or from, say, Berlin or Brussels to Warsaw (EuroCity). The next category is called a *pospieszny* service, which stops at more stations. Seat reservations aren't usually needed for this type of train. The slowest services are called *osobowy*. These slow trains trundle along and stop at every station along the way.
www.pkp.pl

By bus

The national bus service is operated by PKS, which has a depot in almost every town. Buses are often more convenient than the train when making short journeys, and in the mountains of the south the bus may be your only option. Several long-distance routes are operated by Polski Express (e.g. between Warsaw and Kraków). Bus stations are usually found adjacent to the railway station in the vast majority of towns, and tickets can only be bought from ticket offices there. Buying a ticket in advance guarantees you a seat.

By car

Poland's road network and Polish road users are a test of patience even for experienced drivers. Driving on the right (if you are from the UK) will be the least of your worries as you negotiate potholes, traffic jams, rude drivers, drunks, speeding, suicidal

Take care on winter roads

overtaking and fume-belching Ukrainian trucks, not to mention the omnipresent traffic police. Hiring a car is as easy as anywhere in Europe and may be preferable to risking damage to your own.

City transport

Wherever you travel in Poland, city buses, trams, and the metro in Warsaw all use more or less the same system. Tickets must be bought in advance and stamped inside the vehicle (or before going down to the platform in the metro). Simply buying a ticket is not enough – you will be fined if you do not stamp it.

Accommodation

There are almost 7,000 places to stay in Poland, with a total of over half a million beds, making finding accommodation, even in high season, relatively easy. The country now has every type of accommodation you can imagine or require – from 5-star luxury hotels in historical buildings to basic campsites by lakes; and from cosy pensions with embroidered bed covers and home cooking to mountain refuges in the Tatras with log fires and fellow travellers sharing tales.

Whatever your budget, tastes and travel plans, there is always accommodation available to suit your needs. Standards are generally high whatever you choose, and many Polish hotels are either newly built or recently renovated. As in many countries in Central and Eastern Europe, the one sector where improvements could be made is in backpacker hostels, but even here you should experience few problems in major tourist centres such Warsaw and Kraków. Some student hostels welcome paying guests over the summer.

Cost

By far your biggest expense on any trip to Poland will be your accommodation. Hotels are slightly cheaper than in the West, but not incredibly so, while at campsites it may cost just a few złoty to pitch a tent and have a shower. The best value comes at small family-run guesthouses, especially in rural areas. A room for the night at one of these cosy places can cost just a handful of złoty, and the personal touches are thrown in for free. The sky is the limit at luxury hotels in Kraków, Warsaw and other major cities, and you can pay over 1,000 złoty to stay at hotels like the Grand in Sopot or the Copernicus in Kraków. Boutique hotels are thin on the ground, and recent years have seen an enormous growth in the number of soulless business accommodation chains charging a standard rate for every room.

Checking in and paying

On arrival at a hotel, the staff at reception will ask to see your passport, and you may also be required to fill in a form with some basic personal details. In low season, or any other time when the hotel may be experiencing low occupancy rates, ask to see the room before you take it. Requesting a room with a specific view or away from a busy road is acceptable. Apart from the more basic rural establishments away from the main tourist attractions, most hotels will accept payment by major credit or debit card.

Booking

If you are not using a travel agent, booking by telephone is the best way to make a reservation. Here a simple rule applies – if the person at the other end does not speak English, consider whether this is a suitable place for you to stay. However, most hotel staff do speak some English these days. Reserving your hotel over the internet may save you some money and does

not present a risk in Poland, but contact details for the hotel concerned may be hard to find should you have a query about your stay.

Hotels

The situation with hotels in Poland is changing rapidly. An ever-increasing number of 4- and 5-star hotels are being built, while numbers at the bottom end of the market are decreasing. The biggest number of hotels, however, falls into the 3-star category. Poland has its own star system which may not correspond exactly to Western standards. En-suite facilities, daily room cleaning, breakfast and 24-hour reception come

Hotel Bristol, Warsaw

as standard at most hotels, and if you find one where this is not true, go elsewhere. Room rates fall in winter (except around Christmas and New Year) and rise again for the summer season. Some hotels specialising in business clientele may have special weekend rates. Some places may raise their prices during important trade fairs, and you should watch out for this in Poznań in particular.

The vast majority of hotels serve breakfast, and accommodate Western tastes in this respect with full cooked and Continental breakfasts, a foreign concept in Poland. Poles will smoke almost anywhere, and this can be particularly annoying in hotel breakfast rooms. Some hotels have restaurants on the premises, but these can be slightly overpriced.

Guesthouses

Staying at small pensions and family-run guesthouses can be an enjoyable experience and bring you closer to the locals. Standards and facilities vary wildly in this sector and you should always ask to see the room before committing. Some of the best can be found in the Polish countryside, on farms, and in villages on popular hiking routes.

Apartments

In major cities there are usually several agencies that rent out self-contained apartments in attractive locations. These are more suited to visitors staying for long periods of time, but some agencies will accept one-night bookings.

Delfin Hotel, Augustow

The Grand Hotel at Sopot Beach

Hostels

The number of hostels is on the increase, but there is room for more, especially away from the major tourist attractions. Standards are high at most hostels. University accommodation is a cheap option in summer, but standards can be relatively low. Booking ahead is usually necessary in Kraków, Warsaw and Gdańsk in the summer months.

Campsites

Poland has approximately 400 campsites spread around the country. These can be large affairs with shops, restaurants and bungalows for rent, or simply fields with a basic shower block. A camping holiday is one of the cheapest ways to see Poland, but watch out for the mosquitoes in the northern lake belt, which can be a real headache. Camping equipment is available in major cities but hard to source elsewhere. Wild camping is possible outside of national parks and other protected areas.

Mountain refuges

The number of mountain refuges has been falling in recent years. Most are run either by the PTTK or the PZA (Polski Związek Alpinizmu – The Polish Mountaineering Association). You can find a full list of these at *www.turystyka-gorska.pl/ schroniska.php*

Food and drink

Those who think Polish cuisine is all potatoes and sauerkraut will be pleasantly surprised by what is on offer in the country today. Polish fare is without doubt some of the tastiest in Central and Eastern Europe, with some delicious variations on neighbouring cuisines, and influences ranging from Tartar, Armenian and Lithuanian to Cossack, Hungarian and Jewish.

Breakfast is often a quick and light affair of bread, cheese and tea, although hotels cater to Western tastes with full Continental and English breakfasts. Poles then have a snack or second breakfast around lunchtime, and the main meal of the day is eaten at around 4 or 5pm. This can mean that restaurants are empty around the time that most tourists look for lunch.

Gingerbread figures from Toruń

Dinner begins with dripping (*smalec*) on bread, with pickled gherkins as a starter, followed by *Żurek*, a sour rye soup containing a boiled egg or sausage, or *Barszcz*, a clear version of Russian borscht. Typical main dishes include *pierogi* (small dumplings filled with meat, potato, sauerkraut or cheese), *gołąbki* (cabbage leaves stuffed with meat and rice), *golonka* (pig knuckle), duck with apples, *naleśniki* (stuffed pancakes), beef roll with buckwheat, *bigos* (a concoction of sauerkraut and meat) and *kotlet schabowy* (battered pork cutlet). Poles also love mushrooms (*grzyby*), which feature heavily on many menus. For dessert be sure to try Polish cheesecake (*sernik*) or apple cake (*szarlotka*), often served hot with ice cream.

The Poles' favourite fast food used to be *zapiekanka*, a slice of baguette with a cheese, mushroom and ham topping grilled for a couple of minutes into a kind of Polish pizza.

Real pizza, hamburgers, chips and other delights of Western cuisine are slowly taking over.

The Poles drink gallons of tea (*herbata*) every year, and it is by far the most popular hot drink. Black tea dominates, but herbal and fruit teas are growing in popularity. Coffee (*kawa*) is as good as it gets in this part of the world, and the locals also love cocoa. Fruit juices and cola are popular soft drinks.

While vodka is popular among the over 40s, the younger generations are turning to beer (*piwo*). Don't leave Poland without trying a shot of Żubrówka (bison grass vodka) with apple juice, and inexpensive bottles of vodka and Goldwasser make great souvenirs. Poland's beer market, although no match for the Czechs' to the south, is booming. The most common brands are Żywiec, Tyskie,

Cheese for sale in Zakopane

Okocim, Lech, Tatra and Żubr. Your half-litre (just under a pint) of fermented hop juice occasionally comes with complimentary bread, dripping and salt. Polish wine is at best drinkable, and it is produced in tiny quantities in the west of the country, making availability a problem.

Poland has no tipping culture, but rounding the bill up to the nearest 5 or 10 złoty is a simple way of showing you were happy with the food and service. Menus are only occasionally in English.

In summer, many restaurants and cafés provide outdoor seating under huge parasols, more often than not emblazoned with the logo of a popular Polish beer. On most Polish main squares these parasol cities merge into one another, forming an impenetrable barrier between the square and the surrounding houses.

You may need help deciphering the menu!

Polish beer and vodka

Though beer is slowly taking a greater market share, there's nothing the Poles like better than a shot of neat vodka. No visitor to Poland can leave without sampling some, and a few glasses of what must be some of the best vodka in Europe is a quintessentially Polish experience, the equivalent of sipping wine in France or whisky in Scotland. As a visitor you are likely to be offered vodka rather than beer for tradition's sake.

Vodka

Vodka (or *wódka* in Polish) has just as strong a tradition in Polish culture as it does in Russia and Ukraine to the

A brewery in Poznań

east. Vodka comes in many different guises, various-shaped bottles, and with myriad names. Two of the best to look for are Wyborowa and Żubrówka, but there are literally hundreds of others out there of varying standards. Clear vodkas stand on the supermarket and bar shelves alongside a rainbow of others with added flavours. Honey, pepper, black cherries, juniper berries, rowan berries and lemon are just some of the additives, and there is even one available infused with cannabis leaf. Żubrówka is perhaps the most famous as it is infused with bison grass from the forests of the Białowieża National Park. This is traditionally drunk with apple juice in a mix called a *szarlotka*. Poles look upon using vodka in cocktails the same way the Czechs deride the practice of employing fruit juices to flavour beer.

Some brands have histories going back centuries; for instance, the Żubrówka recipe dates back to the 16th century. Many have appeared in the last decade or so in the free-market dash to claim a share of a lucrative market. It is thought that vodka began to be produced as early as the 8th century, but it was

Some local beer and vodka brands

probably used more for medicinal purposes initially.

Vodka is traditionally served neat, although younger Poles may mix it with fruit juices. Glasses are drained in one go, and the vodka is quickly followed by a bite of bread, gherkin or other tasty morsel. Not many visitors can keep this up for long, and none manage to match the Poles in drinking prowess (unless they are from Russia or Ukraine). As a foreign visitor, it is acceptable to sip your vodka in stages or miss a few toasts.

Beer

Poland is not the first country that comes to mind when you think of beer, but the country does have some very drinkable brews. Żywiec, Warka,

Tyskie, Okocim, Lech, Tatra and Żubr are the most celebrated brands, and are becoming increasingly popular as young people in particular turn away from vodka, preferring several half litres of amber nectar on a night out. Beer is available from all bars, restaurants and cafés, but there may be only one brand on tap, and supermarkets sell vast arrays of bottled beer for much lower prices. Beer consumption at present stands at 80 litres (140 pints) per person per year; this is set to rise, but may never be able to compete with the Czechs to the south (160 litres/280 pints!). Of course, you don't have to go to Poland to enjoy Polish beer, with 10 million litres (17 million pints) of Tyskie being sold in the UK in 2007.

Entertainment

Poland has as wide a spectrum of entertainment as any Western European country. Opera and classical music are of a particularly high standard, and folk music represents a truly unique Polish experience.

Less highbrow entertainment is now available in the form of cafés, pubs and restaurants, some of which feature live music. Jazz is popular, even among young people, and most music genres get an airing somewhere in the country. For visitors, the language barrier is a problem at the theatre, but not at the cinema.

Nightlife and eating out

Not that long ago, even a large Polish city would have had only a handful of dimly lit pubs, restaurants (usually within a hotel) and snack bars. How times have changed! In the last decade there has been an explosion of new places to eat, drink and be merry, with countless new watering holes and eateries popping up in every town. Rural-themed restaurants equipped with heavy timber furniture and rustic décor are all the rage these days, as are cosy, cottage-like coffee houses. You will also find classic restaurants with over-the-top formal table settings and

scurrying waiters. Bars range from grungy vodka-stained locals for locals, to trendy neon-lit places full of cutting-edge design. Microbreweries and student bars in places like Wrocław, Poznań and Kraków are great fun and always lively. Nightclubs in Poland can be rowdy affairs, thumping with deafening techno and hip-hop music and full of teenage clubbers. There is a slight lack of more grown-up, calmer venues for a laid-back night out. Poland is still a relatively inexpensive country, and an enjoyable night on the tiles costs a fraction of what you would pay back home.

Cinema and theatre

Visiting the cinema does not present a problem for non-Poles, as hardly any films are dubbed into Polish for the silver screen (alas, not true for TV). Ticket prices are relatively low, and for the bona fide Eastern European cinema experience, choose a city-centre communist-era venue. Out-of-town multi-screen cinemas will be identical to those you have at home.

Theatre is not really an option for visitors from abroad unless they understand Polish. There are occasional English-language theatre productions staged in Warsaw, but they are few and far between.

Opera

Opera productions are of the highest standard in Poland, and ticket prices are affordable. Don't be surprised to see that a large section of the audience is made up of young people in jeans. Opera is still a 'living' art form in Poland and a favourite among students, especially those studying music, and all major cities have an opera venue. Be aware that opera subtitles will be in Polish; some visitors can be taken aback by this quite natural aspect of opera abroad.

Music

The best place in the world to experience a Chopin concert is, of course, the composer's homeland. With so many music students in Poland, classical music performances are of the highest standard, and if you have the chance to attend a performance, don't hesitate. Jazz is becoming increasingly popular, and most towns now have some form of jazz venue. Folk music is most common in the south and east, especially at folk festivals and events.

A full house at the Warsaw Philharmonic

Shopping

Poland has never exactly been a shoppers' paradise, but the situation has improved dramatically in the last few years. Half-empty shops selling pickles, vodka and hefty electrical goods have been replaced with modern glass-and-steel shopping malls housing many of the well-known outlets you may know from the high street or mall back home, although bargains and sales are thin on the ground. Most visitors seek out more traditional articles to take home such as the following.

Alcohol

A bottle of Polish firewater is what weighs down the suitcase of many a tourist leaving Poland. Polish vodka is arguably as good as its counterparts in Russia and Ukraine, and comes in myriad bottles, flavours and qualities. Goldwasser, a herbal liqueur from Gdańsk, is a real novelty tipple as it has flakes of real 22-carat gold suspended in it. It can be purchased throughout Poland. Polish beer is of a very high standard, but may weigh down your luggage, and most varieties can be bought at home anyway.

Shopping street in Warsaw

Amber

Amber can be found on beaches along the Baltic coast. With colours ranging from almost white to dark orange, it can be made into all shapes and sizes of jewellery. Shops and stalls selling amber are a ubiquitous feature of every town and city across Poland. Be careful of fake amber, which is very easy to replicate (*see p104*).

Antiques and art

Gone are the days when semi-valuable antiques could be found lying around in dusty second-hand shops in Central and Eastern Europe. The value of everything is now well documented, and the chances of picking up a bargain minimal. Be aware that you need a permit to export anything made before 9 May 1945. Original art of wildly varying quality can be found in the touristy parts of Poland's cities. Polish poster art is particularly sought-after. In Warsaw, Desa Unicum is a state-run antiques auction house with four sites in the capital.
www.desa.pl

Arts and crafts

The Cepelia chain of shops with outlets across the country is unrivalled when it comes to traditional Polish arts and crafts. Its vast array of ceramics, wicker products, glassware, embroidery and lace makes ideal souvenirs. The Cepelia organisation also supports research in art, handicrafts and ethnography, runs galleries, promotes

Goldwasser from Gdańsk

traditional Polish culture abroad and has a range of other activities. You'll find branches in Warsaw, Kraków and Gdańsk as well as many other smaller towns and cities.
www.cepelia.pl

Books

Glossy coffee-table books abound in Polish bookshops and make fine souvenirs and gifts. Almost every town has an EMPiK bookstore and newsagent where these can be found.

Markets

Almost every city has a market, either covered or out in the open. Gdańsk and Wrocław have impressive covered markets, and Warsaw's Russian market is a sight to behold.

Sport and leisure

Most major sports are now enjoyed across Poland, and the big European favourites are all popular in this country. By far the biggest spectator sport is football (piłka nożna), which draws thousands of spectators to stadiums across the land at weekends. Games popular in Central Europe such as volleyball, basketball and handball are also popular.

On the participatory side, hiking, cycling, climbing and watersports practised on Poland's many lakes and rivers have experienced a boom in the years since the fall of the Iron Curtain. New extreme sports such as snowboarding have also come onto the scene.

Basketball

Basketball (*koszykówka*) is a very popular spectator sport in Poland, and important matches are occasionally televised. The big names in Polish men's basketball are, somewhat surprisingly, the tiny northern towns of Sopot and Wrocławek as well as the larger city of Wrocław. The powerhouses of the women's game are Gdynia and Poznań. In the last decade, the Polish leagues have attracted foreign players from the US and from European basketball superpowers Croatia and Lithuania.

Football

Qualification for the 2006 World Cup put Polish football back on the map after two decades in the wilderness. Although the Polish national team failed to qualify for the second round of matches in Germany, interest was stimulated at home and abroad with gates up for matches across the leagues, and players exported to major Western European clubs. However, Polish football had its heyday in the 1970s and early 1980s when the national team finished third in the World Cups of 1974 and 1982.

The most popular and successful teams in Poland are Legia Warszawa and Wisła Kraków, who have dominated the first division in the last decade. Matches between these two rivals are often the highlight of the Polish football season, but neither has ever set the European Champions League on fire. Other big clubs include Lech Poznań, Cracovia Kraków,

Widzew Łódź, and ŁKS from Łódź. The league system is organised on a pyramid basis with first and second leagues at the top, followed by four regional third divisions and numerous lower regional divisions below them. The first division is currently called the Orange Ekstraklasa. Due to the weather, football takes a winter break from December to March.

Football will be big news in this part of the world in the coming years, as Poland and Ukraine will be the host nations for the 2012 European Championships. This decision heralds the first time that a major football competition will be held in Eastern Europe and has brought together these two large countries in a show of friendship and mutual respect that would have been unthinkable a few short years ago.
Polish Football Association.
www.pzpn.pl

Handball

For those not familiar with this relatively widespread sport in Central and Eastern Europe, it could be described as a sort of five-a-side indoor rugby without tackling played with a small round ball and with miniature football-style goals. Handball (*piłka ręcznej*) is an incredibly fast-moving and exciting sport to watch and is played by men and women across Poland.
Polish Handball Federation.
www.zprp.org.pl

Try horse-riding on the beach

Hiking and mountaineering

Poland has some superb hiking territory, particularly of the lighter variety. The southern uplands are a Mecca for hill walkers, and the country's numerous national parks and forests are also great places to stretch the legs. The Bieszczady, Tatra and Karkonosze mountains provide Poland's finest hill-walking territory, and most places are riddled with well-marked colour-coded hiking trails. Maps are readily available and accommodation usually simple to find. Wild camping is normally acceptable unless you find yourself in a national park or other protected area. Only the highest peaks in the Tatras are good for true mountaineering, but decent mountain days can also be had in the higher reaches of the Karkonosze.

Horse racing

Despite breeding some of the finest horses in Europe, Poland has just two racecourses, in Sopot and Warsaw. Horse racing has never been wildly popular in Central and Eastern Europe, but races outside of the region do sometimes arouse interest.

Ice hockey

Ice hockey (*hokej na lodzie*) is a less popular sport, but there is a strong national league, and the national team often features in the World Championships held every April/May. *Polish Ice Hockey Federation. www.pzhl.org.pl*

Volleyball

Volleyball (*siatkówka*) is another Central and Eastern European indoor favourite with men's and women's leagues. Big teams to watch out for in the men's game are KS Ivett Jastrzębie Borynia from the Silesian town of Jastrzębie Zdrój, and Olsztyn. The women's game is dominated by clubs from Bielsko-Biała and Kalisz. *Polish Volleyball Federation. www.pzps.pl*

Watersports

With so much water sloshing around in its thousands of lakes and washing the northern shores, it is no surprise that watersports are popular in Poland.

You can go windsurfing along the northern coast, or on one of the many lakes in Poland

The Tatra Mountains and the Pieniny Mountains are the best places for rock climbing

The Masurian Lakes, the northern lake belt and the Baltic are the places to go for windsurfing, waterskiing, kayaking, rowing, sailing, diving and swimming.

Winter sports

Although much of Poland is made up of flat plains, skiing is a much-loved sport and leisure activity in the south of the country, especially in the Tatra Mountains and the other ranges that make up the Polish section of the Carpathian arc. Poland's premier ski resort is Zakopane in the Tatra Mountains (*see pp85–6*). Skiing, snowboarding and cross-country skiing are all popular winter sports across the south. In other parts of the country, especially in the north, rosy-cheeked children skating on frozen lakes are a common sight in winter.

Children

Poland may not be the ideal destination for a holiday with children in tow, but there is enough to keep them occupied and content. The country now has an abundance of swimming pools, water parks, zoos, beaches, cinemas, puppet theatres, play centres and toy shops to keep little minds and bodies busy and active. Children enjoy discounts at all museums, tourist sights, places of entertainment and on public transport.

Taking children into restaurants and pubs is usually not a problem, and supermarkets now stock everything you need for even your smallest infants. Cinema is an option in Poland as all films are in their original language with Polish subtitles.

There are some issues you should be aware of before heading to Poland with your entourage. Children should be supervised at all times near Poland's lethal roads. Check all play equipment, especially outdoors, before letting the children loose on it, as health and safety can be lax.

Restaurants and pubs can be very smoky, and Poles have no qualms about lighting up around children. Although this is a wild generalisation, Polish children tend to be quieter and more disciplined than their Western counterparts, and tantrums and other naughty antics will attract attention.

CINEMAS
Kraków
Ars
Kraków's most central cinema.
ul. św. Jana 6, Kraków.
Tel: 012 421 41 99. www.ars.pl

Warsaw
Kinoplex
A centrally located picture house.
Aleja Solidarności 115, Warsaw.
Tel: 022 654 45 45. www.kinoplex.pl
Kinoteka
One of Warsaw's most central cinemas with an amazing Stalinist interior.
Palace of Culture and Science, Warsaw.
Tel: 022 551 70 70. www.kinoteka.pl

PLAYROOMS
Warsaw
Bajlandia
ul. Głębocka 15, Warsaw.
Tel: 022 331 35 90.
Eldorado
ul. Powstańców Śląnskich 126, Warsaw.
Tel: 022 569 79 69.

PUPPET THEATRES
Gdańsk
Miniatura
ul. Grunwaldzka 16, Gdańsk.
Tel: 058 341 12 09.
www.teatrminiatura.pl

Warsaw
Baj
ul. Jagiellońska, Warsaw.
Tel: 022 818 08 21. www.teatrbaj.waw.pl
Guliwer
ul. Różana 16, Warsaw. Tel: 022 845 16
76. www.teatrguliwer.waw.pl
Lalka
Palace of Culture and Science, Warsaw.
Tel: 022 620 49 50.
www.teatrlalka.waw.pl

THEME PARKS
Bałtowski Park Jurajski
If your kids are going through their
'dinosaur phase' they'll love this theme
park in the southeast of the country
featuring 60 life-size dinosaur models.
Bałtów 8a. Tel: 041 264 14 20.
www.baltowskipark.pl

WATER PARKS
Gdańsk
Sopot Aquapark
ul. Zamkowa Góra 3–5, Sopot,
Gdańsk. Tel: 058 555 85 55.
www.aquaparksopot.pl

Kraków
Kraków Aqua Park
ul. Dobrego Pasterza 126, Kraków.
Tel: 012 616 31 90. www.parkwodny.pl

ZOOS
Gdańsk
Oliwa Zoo
ul. Karwieńska 3, Gdańsk.
Tel: 058 552 00 42. www.zoo.gdansk.pl

Kraków
Kraków Zoo
ul. Kasy Oszczednosci 14, Kraków.
Tel: 012 425 35 51. www.zoo-krakow.pl

Poznań
Poznań Zoo
Poznań Zoo is divided into two parts.
New Zoo. ul. Krańcowa 81.
Tel: 061 877 35 17.
Old Zoo. ul. Zwierzyniecka 19.
Tel: 061 848 08 63. www.zoo.poznan.pl

Warsaw
Warsaw Zoo
ul. Ratuszowa 1/3, Warsaw.
Tel: 022 619 40 41. www.zoo.waw.pl

Wrocław
Wrocław Zoo
Often described as Poland's finest zoo.
ul. Wroblewskiego 1–5, Wrocław.
Tel: 071 348 30 24. www.zoo.wroclaw.pl

Deer at Oliwa Zoo in Gdańsk

Essentials

Arriving in Poland
By air

There are direct flights to Polish cities (Bydgoszcz, Gdańsk, Katowice, Kraków, Łódź, Poznań, Rzeszów, Szczecin, Warsaw, Wrocław) from airports around the UK and Ireland (Belfast, Birmingham, Bournemouth, Bristol, Cork, Doncaster, Dublin, East Midlands, Edinburgh, Gatwick, Glasgow, Leeds/Bradford, Liverpool, Luton, Manchester, Shannon, Stansted).

By car

Distances by road to Warsaw from:
Berlin 578km (359 miles)
Brussels 1,315km (817 miles)
Paris 1,586km (986 miles)
Prague 618km (384 miles)
Vienna 692km (430 miles).

By train

There are regular direct international train services from Warsaw to Berlin, Brussels, Cologne, Dresden, Kiev, Leipzig, Minsk, Moscow, Prague and Vilnius. It is possible to travel from London to Warsaw with only two changes using the Eurostar service.

By bus

There are now numerous coach connections between London and most major cities in Poland used by migrant workers. Eurolines runs services to Warsaw and Kraków.

Customs

Travellers needn't declare duty-free articles for personal use. If arriving from a non-EU country, excess duty must be paid if amounts exceed: 200 cigarettes, 50 cigars or 250g of pipe tobacco, 2 litres of still wine, 1 litre of spirits. If arriving from another EU country, excess duty must be paid if amounts exceed: 800 cigarettes, 200 cigars or 1kg of pipe tobacco, 110 litres of beer, 90 litres of still wine and 10 litres of spirits.

Driving
Rental

All major rental companies operate in Poland and have desks at major airports.
Avis
Tel: 22 650 48 69 (Warsaw).
Tel: 12 629 61 08 (Kraków).
Budget
Tel: 22 650 40 62 (Warsaw).
Tel: 12 285 50 25 (Kraków).
Europcar
Tel: 22 650 25 60 (Warsaw).
Tel: 12 633 77 73 (Kraków).
Hertz
Tel: 22 650 28 96 (Warsaw).
Tel: 12 429 62 62 (Kraków).

Roads

Roads are in a poor state in Poland. Traffic jams are common, as are accidents. Often a toll must be paid to use motorways, but these are few and far between. Polish traffic police are notorious for stopping foreign cars.

Roadside assistance

Calling the number *96 37* from anywhere in Poland will get you through to the nearest PZM (Polish Motoring Association) service centre.

Rules

Speed limits are (unless otherwise posted): 60kph (37mph) in built-up areas; 90kph (56mph) on main roads; 110kph (68mph) on expressways; and 130kph (81mph) on motorways. Dipped headlights are mandatory after dark year-round and all day from October to April. Right-hand drive vehicles must have converted headlights. Permissible alcohol content in the blood is 0.2 per cent.

Electricity

Poland works on 220V AC, 50Hz. To use electrical appliances from the UK or the US, you will need a Continental two-pin adaptor.

English-language media

There are two weekly English-language newspapers in Warsaw – *The Warsaw Business Journal* and *The Warsaw Voice*. UK newspapers are hard to come by.

Entry formalities

EU citizens do not need visas to visit Poland, just a passport valid for three months after the date they intend to leave. Citizens of the US, Australia, Canada and New Zealand can stay without a visa for up to 90 days. All other nationals should check with their local Polish embassy.

Money
Currency

The Polish currency is the złoty (pronounced *zwo-ti*), which is divided into 100 groszy. The abbreviations are zł, or PLN, and gr. Notes come in denominations of 200zł, 100zł, 50zł, 20zł and 10zł, and there are 1zł, 2zł, 5zł, 1gr, 2gr, 5gr, 10gr, 20gr and 50gr coins. Poland is not expected to join the Eurozone until 2010 at the earliest.

Credit cards and cheques

Use of credit cards is on the increase, but is still largely limited to petrol stations, upmarket hotels and restaurants, and large supermarket chains. Travellers' cheques can be cashed at many banks, but this is a time-consuming process. Take your passport with you.

Cash machines

Cash machines (ATMs) accepting foreign cards are now fairly common, but not as widespread as in the UK and US.

Changing currency

For the best rates, change your pounds, dollars and euros at *kantors*, small booths on street corners, stations, etc. Make sure all foreign notes are in good order (no rips or missing corners) as cashiers can refuse to accept them. British notes should have nothing written on them. You could change your money into złoty before you leave home, or at banks in Poland, but the exchange rates will be worse than at the *kantors*.

Opening hours

Banks

Open: Mon–Fri 9am–4pm; large city branches Mon–Fri 8am–6pm, Sat 9am–2pm.

Shops

Open: Mon–Fri 10am–6pm, Sat 10am–2pm. Big out-of-town chains usually have Western opening hours.

Pharmacies

All major cities and even minor towns will have several pharmacies (*apteka*). Every town has at least one pharmacy open 24 hours. Addresses can be found in local newspapers.

Post

The postal service is operated by Poczta Polska. Post offices in major cities are open 8am–8pm, some 24 hours. Post boxes are red.

Public holidays

1 January – New Year
March/April – Easter Sunday and Monday
1 May – Labour Day
3 May – Constitution
May/June – Corpus Christi
15 August – Assumption Day
1 November – All Saints' Day
11 November – Independence Day
25, 26 December – Christmas

Sustainable tourism

Thomas Cook is a strong advocate of ethical and fairly traded tourism and believes that the travel experience should be as good for the places visited as it is for the people who visit them. That's why we firmly support The Travel Foundation, a charity that develops solutions to help improve and protect holiday destinations, their environment, traditions and culture. To find out what you can do to make a positive difference to the places you travel to and the people who live there, please visit *www.thetravelfoundation.org.uk*

Tax

If you buy an item in Poland worth more than 200zł, and you are flying out of the EU, you are eligible for a value-added tax (VAT) refund. Present the goods (unused and with the price tags attached), your passport, ticket/boarding pass, Global Refund receipt and the shop receipt to customs at the airport.

Telephones

Telephone services are operated by Telekommunikacja Polska. Card-operated public phone boxes are widespread. All Polish landline numbers must have seven digits.

Country code + *48*
City codes
Gdańsk *058*
Kraków *012*
Łódź *042*
Poznań *061*
Warsaw *022*

(Omit the initial '0' when dialling from abroad.)

Overseas
To dial abroad from Poland:
00 + country code + area code + subscriber number.
Country codes
UK *44*
US and Canada *1*
Ireland *353*
Australia *61*
New Zealand *64*

Time

Poland is on Central European Standard Time which is GMT + 1. This means it is one hour ahead of the UK, six hours ahead of US Eastern Standard Time and ten hours behind Sydney in Australia.

Tipping

Service is included in the bill, but if you are satisfied with the level of service, round up the bill to the nearest 5 złoty.

Toilets

Toilets have improved dramatically in Poland in the last few years, and most are now of a good standard. Men's and women's are marked with an upside-down triangle and a circle respectively. Public toilets are never free of charge, so expect to pay at least 1zł to spend a penny.

Tourist information

The majority of large and medium-size towns have a tourist information office ranging from spartan, threadbare affairs with no information to well-stocked operations with brochures on absolutely every aspect of the town or region. In Warsaw, there are official tourist information booths at the airport, the Old Town, the main railway station and the bus station. In Kraków, they can be found on the main square, in the Jewish quarter and near the main railway station.

Travellers with disabilities

Public transport can pose difficulties for travellers with disabilities, especially trains and trams. The situation with disabled access is improving slowly, but many cities are not particularly wheelchair-friendly places. Disabled toilets are slowly being introduced. Upmarket hotels have good disabled facilities, as do some better restaurants.

Language

English is spoken in the major tourist centres such as Warsaw and Kraków, but just a little off the beaten track, people in hotels and restaurants may speak only Polish and perhaps a little German and Russian. Learning a few basic phrases in Polish is a good idea wherever you are heading. Although words may look impossible to pronounce, Polish is a logical language, and each letter or group of letters is almost always pronounced in the same way.

BASIC PHRASES

Hello	Dzień dobry
Goodbye	Do widzenia
Yes	Tak
No	Nie
Please	Proszę
Thank you	Dziękuję
Excuse me	Przepraszam
My name is...	Mam na imię...
Waiter/waitress!	Kelner/Kelnerka!

QUESTIONS

Where is...?	Gdzie jest...?
When?	Kiedy?
How long?	Jak długo?
What time?	O której godzinie?
How much is this?	Ile to kosztuje?
Can I try this on?	Czy mogę to przymierzyć?
May I have the bill, please?	Poproszę o rachunek?
Where is the toilet, please?	Przepraszam, gdzie jest toaleta?
Do you speak English?	Czy mówi Pan/Pani po angielsku?

NUMBERS

Zero	Zero	**Five**	Pięć	**Ten**	Dziesięć
One	Jeden	**Six**	Sześć	**One hundred**	Sto
Two	Dwa	**Seven**	Siedem	**One thousand**	Tysiąc
Three	Trzy	**Eight**	Osiem		
Four	Cztery	**Nine**	Dziewięć		

USEFUL WORDS

Hotel	Hotel
Train	Pociąg
Railway station	Dworzec kolejowy
Bus	Autobus
Bus station	Dworzec autobusowy
Tram	Tramwaj
Plane	Samolot
Airport	Lotnisko
Restaurant	Restauracja
Embassy	Ambasada
Hospital	Szpital
Internet café	Kawiarnia internetowa
Police station	Posterunek policji
Post office	Poczta
Tourist information centre	Biuro informacji turystycznej

DAYS OF THE WEEK

Monday	Poniedziałek
Tuesday	Wtorek
Wednesday	Środa
Thursday	Czwartek
Friday	Piątek
Saturday	Sobota
Sunday	Niedziela

EMERGENCIES

Help!	Na pomoc!
Call a doctor/the police	Proszę wezwać lekarza/policję
Fire!	Pożar!
Stop!	Stop!

Emergencies

Emergency numbers
Ambulance: *999*
Fire brigade: *998*
Police: *997*
Emergency number from mobile
phones: *112*

Health, safety and crime
Health and safety have come on in
leaps and bounds in recent years.
Food hygiene is generally no longer
an issue as restaurants and cafés
must now comply with EU regulation.
Tap water is safe to drink, although it
may not taste very nice.

Road safety *is* an issue, and the
greatest of care must be taken
when crossing the road, never
mind when driving along it. If you
can use public transport, do so,
as few Western drivers will be
prepared for Poland's diabolic
roads and abysmal drivers.

The standard of health care is good
and improving all the time, but it's not
quite up to Western standards in the
public sector yet. Private clinics and
hospitals may offer a better standard
of services than public facilities in the
West, but you will be charged more for
treatment. Paramedical services and
facilities are basic by Western
standards.

There are two types of police
officers in Poland – national and
municipal. If you come into contact

with either, after having something
stolen, for instance, you will find they
do their job – just don't expect cups
of tea and sympathy.

Despite Eastern Europe's
reputation as a crime-ridden
place, actual crime rates are, in all
likelihood, lower than in your home
town. Watch out for pickpockets, bag
snatchers and camera swipers,
especially where large crowds of
tourists congregate. Theft from
vehicles is common, so don't leave
items displayed in your car. At night,
stick to well-lit streets and never
accept lifts from unofficial taxis.

Embassies and consulates
UK
Warsaw Corporate Centre, 2nd Floor,
Emilii Plater 28, 00-688 Warsaw.
Tel: 022 311 00 00.
US
al. Ujazdowskie 29/31, 00-540 Warsaw.
Tel: 022 504 20 00.
Canada
ul. Jana Matejki 1/5, 00-481 Warsaw.
Tel: 022 584 31 00.
Australia
3rd Floor, Nautilus Building,
ul. Nowogrodzka 11, 00-513 Warsaw.
Tel: 022 521 34 44.
New Zealand
Dom Dochodowy, Level 5,
al. Ujazdowskie 51, 00-536 Warsaw.
Tel: 022 521 05 00.

Directory

Accommodation price guide

Prices of accommodation are based on a double room per night for two people sharing, with breakfast.

★	up to 200zł
★★	200–400zł
★★★	400–600zł
★★★★	over 600zł

Eating out price guide

Prices are based on an average three-course meal for one, without drinks.

★	up to 30zł
★★	30–60zł
★★★	60–100zł
★★★★	over 100zł

WARSAW

ACCOMMODATION

Hotel Praski ★/★★

Try something different and stay on the right bank of the Vistula River in the Praga district, just 1km (²/₃ mile) from the Old Town across the bridge. An excellent standard of service for a 2-star establishment. Some rooms have shared bathroom facilities.
al. Solidarności 61.
Tel: 022 201 63 00.
Email: rez@praski.pl.
www.praski.pl

Campanile ★★

This hotel has decent rooms and spotless bathrooms. The city-centre location near the Palace of Culture and Science may not be to everyone's liking.
ul. Towarowa 2.
Tel: 022 582 72 00.
Email: warszawa@ campanile.com.pl.
www.campanile.com.pl

Hotel Mazowiecki ★★

Basic rooms but a great location near the Old Town.
ul. Mazowiecka 10.
Tel: 022 687 91 17.
Email: rezerwacja@ mazowiecki.com.pl.
www.mazowiecki.com.pl

Bristol Hotel ★★★★

Built in 1899, this is arguably Poland's most sumptuous hotel. Luxurious rooms, impeccable service and exclusive hospitality come as standard. Excellent location near the Old Town.
ul. Krakowskie Przedmieście 42/44.
Tel: 022 551 10 00.
www.lemeridien-bristol.com

EATING OUT

Bar Mleczny Pod Barbakanem ★

One of the best-located snack bars in Poland, situated in the Old Town. Expect cheap and cheerful dishes in a no-frills environment for a few złoty. A thoroughly Polish experience.
ul. Mostowa 27/29.
Tel: 022 831 47 37.

Chłopskie Jadło ★★

This rural theme restaurant also has popular branches in Gdańsk and Kraków. Expect lots of hefty timber benches, jars of pickles, ancient agricultural implements and garlands of garlic adorning the bright turquoise walls, as well as a meat-heavy traditional Polish menu.

pl. Konstytucji 1.
Tel: 022 339 17 17.

Restauracja pod Samsonem ★★

Possibly the best place in the New Town to sample real Polish fare with a hint of Jewish influence. Popular, and deservedly so.

ul. Freta 3/5.
Tel: 022 831 17 88.

Fabryka Trzciny ★★★

A marvellous modern restaurant at the Fabryka Trzciny arts centre in the Praga district of the city. The menu features Polish and international fare, and the service is impeccable.

ul. Otwocka 14.
Tel: 022 619 17 05.
Email: restauracja@ fabryka.waw.pl.
www.fabrykatrzciny.pl

ENTERTAINMENT

Fabryka Trzciny (Nightclub)

A great little nightlife spot in the Praga district housed in a former factory building.

ul. Otwocka 14.
Tel: 022 619 05 13.
www.fabrykatrzciny.pl

Ice Bar (Nightclub)

One room is just a normal bar, but the other is kept at –8°C and is equipped with tables, seating, a bar, shot glasses and pieces of sculpture made entirely of ice!

ul. Pańska 61.
Tel: 022 654 56 34.
www.icebar.com.pl

Kinoteka (Cinema)

Centrally located in the tallest building in the country.

Palace of Culture and Science. Tel: 022 826 19 61.
www.kinoteka.pl

Metro Jazz Club

A cool club in the city centre.

Hotel Metropol,
ul. Marszałkowska 99A.
Tel: 022 629 40 00.
www.hotelmetropol.com.pl

National Philharmonic (Classical music)

ul. Jasna 5.
Tel: 022 55 17 128.
www.filharmonia.pl

Tygmont (Jazz)

Listed as one of the top 100 jazz venues in the world.

Mazowiecka 6–8.
Tel: 022 828 34 09.
www.tygmont.com.pl

Warsaw Chamber Opera

al. Solidarności 76.

Tel: 022 831 22 40.
www.operakameralna.pl

Warsaw Grand Theatre (Opera)

The capital's premier opera venue.

Plac Teatralny 1.
Tel: 022 692 05 08.
www.teatrwielki.pl

SPORT AND LEISURE

City Tennis Club

Wybrzeże Kościuszkowskie 2.
Tel: 022 821 43 43.

First Warsaw Golf and Country Club

A 27-hole course north of the capital.

Rajszew 70.
Tel: 022 782 45 55.
www.warsawgolf.pl

Horse-riding

A comprehensive list of riding centres and clubs can be found at *www.jazdakonna.pl.* The site is in Polish, but the interactive map is self-explanatory.

Legia Warszawa (Football)

Stadium.
ul. Łazienkowska 3.
www.legia.com

Sluzewiec Racetrack (Horse racing)

ul. Pulawska 266.
Tel: 022 843 11 32.

Tennis

Poland's most important international tennis tournament is the J&S Cup which is part of the WTA Tour. The event is held in Warsaw in early May.
Polish Tennis Federation. www.pzt.pl

Wagabunda Bike Rental

As well as cycle hire, Wagabunda also offers cycling tours of Warsaw.
ul. Czackiego 3–5.
Tel: 060 585 84 58.
www.wagabunda.com

THE NORTHEAST
Mikołajki
SPORT AND LEISURE

Wioska Żeglarska (Watersports)

Wioska Żeglarska is a boat hire company.
ul. Kowalska 3.
Tel: 668 442 042.
www.wioskazeglarskamiko lajki.pl

MAŁOPOLSKA AND THE CARPATHIAN MOUNTAINS
Kraków
ACCOMMODATION

Eden ★★

Located in the Kazimierz district, this hotel focuses on a Jewish clientele. It has the only functioning Mikveh (ritual bath) in Poland and Kraków's only genuine kosher restaurant. Housed in three 15th-century town houses, it has a modern interior.
ul. Ciemna 15.
Tel: 012 430 65 65.
Email: eden@hoteleden.pl.
www.hoteleden.pl

Hotel Polonia ★★

You will see this large hotel on leaving the railway station. Rooms are spacious and airy with high ceilings.
ul. Basztowa 25.
Tel: 012 422 12 33.
Email: rezerwacja@ hotel-polonia.com.pl.
www.hotel-polonia.com.pl

Saski ★★

A magical old hotel and a fitting place to stay in Kraków. The standard rooms do what they say on the tin, but the suites have little rococo flourishes as well as all mod cons.
ul. Sławkowska 3.
Tel: 012 421 42 22. Email: info@hotelsaski.com.pl.
www.hotelsaski.com.pl

Hotel Wawel-Tourist ★★★

With an excellent location just off Grodzka Street, 200m (220yds) from Wawel Castle, the Wawel-Tourist offers good value for money in the heart of the historical centre.
ul. Poselska 22.
Tel: 012 424 13 00. Email: hotel@hotelwawel.pl.
www.wawel-tourist.com.pl

Copernicus ★★★★

The crème-de-la-crème of accommodation options in Kraków with room rates to match. The 29 five-star rooms do not disappoint, and neither does the swimming pool in the basement. Fine location near Wawel Castle.
ul. Kanonicza 16.
Tel: 012 424 34 00. Email: copernicus@hotel.com.pl.
www.hotel.com.pl/ copernicus

Maltański ★★★★

The Maltański is a wonderfully cosy boutique hotel just a few steps outside the historical centre. Beautiful rooms, helpful staff and a real feeling of being looked after – priceless in touristy Kraków.
ul. Straszewskiego 14.
Tel: 012 431 00 10.
Email: maltanski@ donimirski.com.
www.donimirski.com

EATING OUT

Jadłodajnia ★

This has been a budget eatery in the centre of Kraków since 1934. Traditional everyday Polish fare for the masses.
ul. Sienna 11.
Tel: 012 421 14 44. Open: almost 24 hours.

Nostalgia ★★

A traditional Polish restaurant with rural décor and a wide range of dishes on the menu.
ul. Karmelicka 10.
Tel: 012 425 42 60.

Smak Ukraiński ★★

A good introduction to traditional fare from Poland's eastern neighbour.
ul. Kanonicza 15.
Tel: 012 421 92 94.
www.ukrainska.pl

ENTERTAINMENT

Karol Szymanowski Philharmonic in Kraków (Classical music)

Home to the famous Kraków Philharmonic Orchestra.
ul. Zwierzyniecka 1.
Tel: 012 422 94 77. www. filharmonia.krakow.pl

Pasaż (Cinema)

World cinema on Kraków's main square.
Rynek Glowny 9.
Tel: 012 422 77 13.

Piec Art (Jazz)

One of the slickest jazz joints in Kraków. Wednesday night is live music night.
ul. Szewska 12.
Tel: 12 429 64 25.
www.piec.krakow.pl

SPORT AND LEISURE

Eskada Sports and Recreation Centre (Tennis)

ul. Szuwarowa 1.
Tel: 012 262 76 47.

Kraków Valley Golf & Country Club

A fine course near Kraków.
Paczółtowice 328.
Tel: 012 258 60 00.
www.valley.mv.net.pl

Rentabike (Cycling)

A respectable cycle hire company that offers 24-hour service.
Tel: 888 029 792.

Wisła Kraków (Football)

Stadium: ul. Reymonta 22.
www.wisla.krakow.pl

Zakopane

ACCOMMODATION

Sabała ★★

Some rooms here give the impression that you are staying at a cosy mountain lodge, with their timber ceilings and traditional wooden furniture. This is Zakopane's oldest hotel and dates from 1897.
ul. Krupówki 11.
Tel: 018 201 50 92.
Email: recepcja@ sabala.zakopane.pl.
www.sabala.zakopane.pl

Villa Marilor ★★★

This renovated 19th-century villa in the centre of Zakopane contains one of the town's best hotels.
ul. Kościuszki 18.
Tel: 018 200 06 70.
Email: rezerwacja@ hotelmarilor.com.
www.hotelmarilor.com

POMERANIA AND WIELKOPOLSKA

Gdańsk

ACCOMMODATION

Dom Muzyka ★★

A newly created cheap and cheerful place, a short walk from the historical centre. Spick and span rooms and English-speaking staff.
ul. Łąkowa 1/2.
Tel: 058 326 06 00. Email: biuro@dom-muzyka.pl.
www.dom-muzyka.pl

Hotel Królewski ★★

Housed in a rebuilt granary on Ołowianka Island, the 30 smart rooms

are of a higher standard
than the room rate
suggests. There are pretty
views of Gdańsk's old
centre from the upper
floors and an excellent
restaurant on the
premises.
ul. Ołowianka 1.
Tel: 058 326 11 11. Email:
office@hotelkrolewski.pl.
www.hotelkrolewski.pl
Podewils ★★★★
A seriously stylish hotel on
the banks of the Motława
River. Possibly the best
place to stay in Gdańsk.
ul. Szafarnia 2.
Tel: 058 300 95 60.
www.podewils-hotel.pl

EATING OUT
Pi Kawa ★
Open the door of this
small coffee house in
Piwna Street and smell the
strong coffee aroma that
perfumes the air. One of
the best places in Gdańsk
for coffee and cakes.
ul. Piwna 5–6.
Tel: 058 309 14 44.
Open: 10am–midnight.
Swojski Smak ★★
The focus here is on
simple hearty Polish
dishes that warm your
insides on cold days. The
huge country portions

are excellent value, and
the rural theme a lot
of fun.
ul. Heweliusza 25/27.
Tel: 058 320 19 12.
www.swojskismak.pl.
Open: Mon–Fri noon–
10pm, Sat & Sun 1–10pm.
Gdańska ★★★
This Gdańsk institution
can seat up to 220 people
in five halls, each one
more elaborately fitted
out than the next.
Enjoy hearty Polish fare
among the antiques and
over-the-top décor.
ul. Św. Ducha 16–24.
Tel: 058 305 76 71.
www.gdanska.pl.
Open: noon–midnight.

ENTERTAINMENT
Baltic Opera
al. Zwyciestwa 15.
Tel: 058 763 49 12.
www.operabaltycka.pl
Cinema City Krewetka
Eight screens of movie
magic in the very heart
of Gdańsk.
ul. Karmelicka 1.
Tel: 58 769 30 00.
**Polish Baltic
Philharmonic
(Classical music)**
The best venue and
orchestra in the north.
ul. Ołowianka 1.

Tel: 058 320 62 62.
www.filharmonia.gda.pl

SPORT AND LEISURE
Joytrip (Watersports)
Joytrip can organise any
activity in or on the Baltic.
ul. Fieldorfa 11/3,
Sopot, Gdańsk.
Tel: 058 320 61 69.
www.joytrip.pl
Rowerownia (Cycling)
Rowerownia hires all
kinds of cycles for biking
around the Tri-City.
Bitwy pod Płowcami 39,
Sopot, Gdańsk.
Tel: 058 320 61 69.
www.rowerownia.gda.pl
**Sopot Hippodrome
(Horse racing)**
ul. Polna 1,
Sopot, Gdańsk.
Tel: 058 551 66 82.
www.skj-sopot.pl
Sopot Tennis Club
ul. Ceynowy 5, Sopot,
Gdańsk. Tel: 058 551 35
69. www.skt.com.pl

Poznań
ACCOMMODATION
Prices in Poznań rise
during large trade fairs.

Hotel Brovaria ★★
The location could not be
better, as this small hotel
is contained within a

typical town house on the main square. Good value for money and home to Poznań's only microbrewery.
Stary Rynek 73/74.
Tel: 061 858 68 68. Email: brovaria@brovaria.pl. www.brovaria.pl

Młyńskie Koło ★★
Some way out of the centre but worth it for the rooms full of dark timber furniture and artwork, as well as the atmospheric restaurant. This timber lodge is not your run-of-the-mill hotel.
ul. Browarna 37.
Tel: 061 878 99 35. Email: gospoda@mlynskiekolo.pl. www.mlynskiekolo.pl

Domina Poznań Residence ★★★★
These top-class serviced apartments are a little bit special with all mod cons and ultra-attentive staff. Quite centrally located.
ul. Św. Marcin 2.
Tel: 061 859 05 90. Email: prestige@dominahotels.pl. www.dominahotels.com

EATING OUT
Brovaria ★★
A newly opened eatery that brews its own beer and serves modern Polish and international dishes. Very popular.
Stary Rynek 73/74.
Tel: 061 858 68 68.

ENTERTAINMENT
Blue Note Jazz Club
Poznań's top jazz venue, attracting some of the biggest acts.
ul. Kościuszki 76–77.
Tel: 061 657 07 77.
www.bluenote.poznan.pl

Grand Theatre (Opera)
Classical venue.
ul. Fredry 9.
Tel: 061 659 02 80.
www.opera.poznan.pl

Multikino (Cinema)
Eight-screen multiplex in the city centre.
ul. Królowej Jadwigi 51.
Tel: 061 835 33 44.
www.multikino.pl

SPORT AND LEISURE
Binowo Park (Golf)
A Swedish-owned course in the northwest of the country with an 18-hole Championship course and a 9-hole practice course.
Binowo 62 (near Szczecin, northwest of Poznań).
Tel: 091 404 15 33.
www.binowopark.pl

Toruń
ACCOMMODATION
Hotel Pod Orłem ★
A more basic option in one of Toruń's oldest hotels. Good room rates for its Old Town location.
ul. Mostowa 17.
Tel: 056 622 50 25. Email: rezerwacja@hotel.torun.pl. www.hotel.torun.pl

Hotel Gotyk ★★
This restored town-house hotel has rooms that are a mix of old and modern. Excellent location.
ul. Piekary 20.
Tel: 056 648 40 00. Email: hotel@hotel-gotyk.com.pl. www.hotel-gotyk.com.pl

Hotel Pod Czarną Różą ★★
Without doubt one of the best mid-range places to stay in Toruń. Every piece of furniture in this old town house seems to be an antique, and the staff are very obliging. The location is good too, just 100m (110yds) from the Old Town Square.
ul. Rabiańska 11.
Tel: 056 621 96 37. Email: hotel@hotelczarnaroza.pl. www.hotelczarnaroza.pl

EATING OUT

Karczma U Sołtysa ★★

A traditional inn serving hearty Polish food.

ul. Mostowa 17.
Tel: 056 652 26 56.

SILESIA

Wrocław

ACCOMMODATION

Dwór Polski ★★

The 'Polish Court' is situated just off the main square and has rooms of a decent standard. Housed in a period building, Polish King Sigmund III is said to have stayed here.

ul. Kiełbaśnicza 2.
Tel: 071 372 34 15.
Email: reception@
dworpolski.wroclaw.pl.
www.
dworpolski.wroclaw.pl

Hotel Patio ★★

A smart, no-nonsense, centrally located hotel near the main square.

ul. Kiełbaśnicza 24.
Tel: 071 375 04 00. Email:
hotel@hotelpatio.pl.
www.hotelpatio.pl

Hotel Tumski ★★

A pretty town house on one of the city's river islands near the cathedral is the scene for this superb hotel. The rooms

are as good as the location.

Wyspa Słodowa 10.
Tel: 071 322 60 88.
Email: hotel@hotel-
tumski.com.pl.
www.hotel-tumski.com.pl

EATING OUT

Spiż Brewery ★★/★★★

An extremely popular microbrewery-cum-pub-cum-eatery under the town hall. Often packed out every night from Wednesday to Saturday. Without doubt one of the best places to eat and drink in the city, and the location could not be more central.

Rynek-Ratusz 9.
Tel: 071 344 72 25.

ENTERTAINMENT

Filharmonia Wrocławska (Classical music)

One of the best classical music venues in Silesia.

ul. Piłsudskiego 19.
Tel: 071 342 24 59. www.
filharmonia.wroclaw.pl

Helios (Cinema)

Latest film releases on nine screens.

ul. Kazimierza
Wielkiego 19a.
Tel: 071 786 65 66.
www.heliosnet.pl

Kino Atom (Cinema)

A Hollywood-free zone. Films from around the world screened in their original language with Polish subtitles.

ul. Piłsudskiego 74.
Tel: 071 347 14 65.
www.acf.pl

Ragtime (Jazz)

Centrally located on the Salt Market, this is one of the best places in Silesia for a jazzy night out.

plac Solny 17.
Tel: 071 343 37 01.

Wrocław Opera

Silesia's top opera house.

ul. Świdnicka 35.
Tel: 071 370 88 18.
www.opera.wroclaw.pl

SPORT AND LEISURE

Basketball

For information on where to see basketball games, go to the Polish Basketball Federation website: *www.pzkosz.pl*

Toya Golf & Country Club

One of the country's most beautiful courses, with 27 holes.

ul. Rakowa 5, Kryniczno (just outside Wrocław).
Tel: 071 388 76 00.
www.toyagolf.pl

Index

Acknowledgements

Thomas Cook Publishing wishes to thank the photographer, CHRISTOPHER HOLT, for the loan of the photographs reproduced in this book, to whom the copyright in the photographs belongs (except the following):
MARC DI DUCA 5, 25, 28, 29, 30, 31, 34, 60, 61, 63, 64, 65, 66, 67, 93, 94, 95, 97, 112, 113, 117, 120, 121, 127, 133, 147B, 149, 153
POLISH NATIONAL TOURIST OFFICE 7, 12, 13, 15, 27, 32, 33, 35, 36, 37, 41, 47, 48, 51, 70, 74, 84, 88, 92, 98, 99, 126, 132, 135, 137, 138, 140, 148, 155, 156, 157
MAREK WOJCIECHOWSKI 49, 53, 54, 56, 78, 86, 89, 96, 116, 129, 131
PICTURES COLOUR LIBRARY 145
WORLD PICTURES/PHOTOSHOT 1, 19, 91
FOTOLIA/ANDREA SEAMANN 144
DREAMSTIME.COM/ROBERT ZYWUCKI 151

For CAMBRIDGE PUBLISHING MANAGEMENT LTD:

Project editor: Robert Wilkinson
Typesetter: Julie Crane
Copy editor: Joanne Osborne
Proofreader: Jan McCann
Indexer: Karolin Thomas

SEND YOUR THOUGHTS TO
BOOKS@THOMASCOOK.COM

We're committed to providing the very best up-to-date information in our travel guides and constantly strive to make them as useful as they can be. You can help us to improve future editions by letting us have your feedback. If you've made a wonderful discovery on your travels that we don't already feature, if you'd like to inform us about recent changes to anything that we do include, or if you simply want to let us know your thoughts about this guidebook and how we can make it even better – we'd love to hear from you.

Send us ideas, discoveries and recommendations today and then look out for your valuable input in the next edition of this title.

Emails to the above address, or letters to Travellers Series Editor, Thomas Cook Publishing, PO Box 227, Unit 9, Coningsby Road, Peterborough PE3 8SB, UK.

Please don't forget to let us know which title your feedback refers to!